FOR THE IB PYP

Wellbeing

Teaching for Success

Dr Kimberley O'Brien

Although every effort has been made to ensure that website addresses are correct at time of going to press, Hodder Education cannot be held responsible for the content of any website mentioned in this book. It is sometimes possible to find a relocated web page by typing in the address of the home page for a website in the URL window of your browser.

Hachette UK's policy is to use papers that are natural, renewable and recyclable products and made from wood grown in well-managed forests and other controlled sources. The logging and manufacturing processes are expected to conform to the environmental regulations of the country of origin.

Orders: please contact Bookpoint Ltd, 130 Park Drive, Milton Park, Abingdon, Oxon OX14 4SE. Telephone: +44 (0)1235 827827. Fax: +44 (0)1235 400401. Email education@bookpoint.co.uk Lines are open from 9 a.m. to 5 p.m., Monday to Saturday, with a 24-hour message answering service. You can also order through our website: www.hoddereducation.com

ISBN: 978 1 5104 8160 2

© Dr Kimberley O'Brien 2020

First published in 2020 by

Hodder Education,
An Hachette UK Company
Carmelite House
50 Victoria Embankment
London EC4Y 0DZ

www.hoddereducation.com

Impression number   10 9 8 7 6 5 4 3 2 1

Year   2024 2023 2022 2021 2020

All rights reserved. Apart from any use permitted under UK copyright law, no part of this publication may be reproduced or transmitted in any form or by any means, electronic or mechanical, including photocopying and recording, or held within any information storage and retrieval system, without permission in writing from the publisher or under licence from the Copyright Licensing Agency Limited. Further details of such licences (for reprographic reproduction) may be obtained from the Copyright Licensing Agency Limited, www.cla.co.uk

Cover photo © pingpao - stock.adobe.com

Illustrations by D'Avila Illustration Agency Ltd

Typeset in India by Aptara Inc.

Printed in Slovenia

A catalogue record for this title is available from the British Library.

Contents

	Acknowledgments	iv
	Introduction	1
Chapter 1	The importance of wellbeing and SEL	4
Chapter 2	Wellbeing and the Learner Profile	16
Chapter 3	ATL skills	40
Chapter 4	ATL skills: Social skills	45
Chapter 5	ATL skills: Communication skills	56
Chapter 6	ATL skills: Self-management skills	65
Chapter 7	Anxiety, stress and mindfulness	75
Chapter 8	Conclusion	85
	Learner Profile worksheets	88
	Bibliography	112
	Index	115

Acknowledgments

This book is dedicated to my two funniest and favourite educators: Mr Wesley Chia (Year 5), for introducing me to the concept of laughing while learning and Mr Paul Wakeling (Year 7), for using humour to lower defence mechanisms and bring individuals together.

I would also like to thank So-Shan Au (Hodder Education, UK) for her original concept, Leonardo Rocker for fostering the connection between Hodder Education and Quirky Kid, Rachel Nickolds and the editing team for their suggestions and Helen Dyer for ensuring more educators and their students have access to the content around the globe. My heartfelt appreciation is also extended to the Lambert family in New Zealand for the writer's haven they unintentionally created in the summer of 2019. Thanks also to Olivia Rocker (13) for generously sharing photographs of her journal activities in these pages, and to Benjamin Rocker (9) for his drawings.

The Publishers would like to thank the following for permission to reproduce copyright material.

The IB Learner Profile and ATL skills © International Baccalaureate Organization.

Photo credits

p.8 © Imaginechina Limited/Alamy Stock Photo, **p.10** *l* © Dr Kimberley O'Brien, **p.12** © Diego cervo/stock.adobe.com, **p.14** © Mutarider15/stock.adobe.com, **p.21** © WavebreakMediaMicro/stock.adobe.com, **p.23** © 4th Life Photography/stock.adobe.com, **p.24** and **p.95** © Moneti/stock.adobe.com, **p.26** © Lorelyn Medina/stock.adobe.com, **p.27** © Nuvolanevicata/stock.adobe.com, **p.29** © Maskot/Getty Images, **p.30** © Munchkinmoo/stock.adobe.com, **pp.33–4** and **pp.104–5** © Macrovector/stock.adobe.com, **p.35** *t* and **p.106** © Pizzastereo/stock.adobe.com, **p.37** and **p.109** © Olivia Rocker, **p.38** and **p.110** © Natalia/stock.adobe.com, **p.40** © Ayelet_keshet/stock.adobe.com, **p.41** © Kakigori Studio/stock.adobe.com, **p.42** © Brocreative/stock.adobe.com, **p.44** © Iryna/stock.adobe.com, **p.47** © Monkey Business/stock.adobe.com, **p.48** *both* © Dr Kimberley O'Brien, **p.51** © Pete Souza – White House via CNP/BJ Warnick/Newscom/Alamy Stock Photo, **p.53** © Angela Hampton Picture Library/Alamy Stock Photo, **p.55** © Dr Kimberley O'Brien, **p.62** © Vlada Loshchenko/Shutterstock.com, **p.64** © Rob z/stock.adobe.com, **p.65** © Blphoto/Alamy Stock Photo, **p.70** © ONYXprj/stock.adobe.com, **p.74** *l* © 2019 UpLoad Publishing Pty Ltd www.upload.com.au, **p.76** © Jacky Chapman/Janine Wiedel Photolibrary/Alamy Stock Photo, **p.83** © Torychemistry/Shutterstock.com, **p.84** © WavebreakMediaMicro/stock.adobe.com

Introduction

Working with children is a pleasure shared by pediatricians, educators and only a handful of other professions dedicated to children's health and wellbeing. We interact with young people on a daily basis, but educators have the added advantage of observing children in groups, often managing social and emotional issues as they arise in classrooms and playgrounds worldwide.

This privilege brings with it extra responsibility and effort on the part of the educator. Navigating the wellbeing of students when things go awry requires a significant emotional investment. It can be exhausting and incredibly rewarding. This unique experience provides the opportunity to make a lifelong impact on the social and emotional wellbeing of a young person, in addition to fostering academic achievement.

To this day, the teachers I recall most fondly are the ones that made me laugh. In primary school, Mr Chia's academic standards were high, but his humour brought the class together. He told a joke at the end of every Monday morning at assembly and I remember the whole school walking away with a smile. As a group of 11-year-olds, we were in tune with his non-verbal cues and his body language. When he stood straight with his hands behind his back, we listened. Mr Chia's style was clear and intentional.

In my first year of secondary school, Mr Wakeling made a similar impression on me. He was witty, firm about his boundaries and, unlike many of my other educators, Mr Wakeling would not tolerate put-downs from one student to another. There were no snickers, sighing or subtle eye rolls between peers if someone gave an incorrect answer. Mr Wakeling would pick up on any negativity immediately. It was never ignored. As a result, everyone's ideas were valued. For a bunch of 13-year-olds who had recently been accepted into this Sydney-based selective school with a competitive entrance exam, the respect and acceptance Mr Wakeling generated was a rare, safe haven for optimal learning.

Another learning environment that left a lasting impression occurred when I set myself free and went backpacking after completing six years of study to become a registered Educational and Developmental Psychologist. At last I was learning in the outdoors, engaging with people, observing new cultures, asking questions, drawing pictures with children and keeping a journal. Learning was fun and I recognized that same feeling I had in classrooms where teachers employed humour – I learn more when I am socially and emotionally satisfied.

This sparked my interest in the social and emotional experiences of students and teachers around the world. In Ghana, West Africa, I met one committed teacher, who hadn't been paid for months, rounding up a group of 50 students with a long cane around a vast playground. The facial expressions of the students suggested their experience of learning was being negatively impacted by their teacher's depleted sense of wellbeing, despite her admirable dedication to the job.

In contrast, playground observations in Cuba featured a backdrop of parents and teachers interacting around the edges of a courtyard filled with happy students and music. They jumped rope, and played chess and clapping games before heading into classrooms to learn languages and musical instruments. The pride of the teachers and enthusiasm from the parent community contributed to the social and emotional wellbeing of the students.

Almost two decades and more than 2 000 school observations later, I find myself aligned with the International Baccalaureate (IB) and the value it places on positive teacher–student relations, whereby 'teachers value students for who they are – their personal and cultural identities, home and family languages, and their prior experiences and learning' (The Learning Community, PYP Programme, 2018, page 12). This feels respectful and intuitive to me.

The wellbeing of teachers is also prioritized in the IB by encouraging 'mutually rewarding and productive relationships' with students, colleagues, parents and the local community. What a great way to make a social impact! This book provides practical strategies for educators to foster social and emotional learning (SEL) among their students. Case examples are used to illustrate how emotions influence behaviour and what educators can do to encourage individuals and groups to self-regulate.

By *'reaching out* to consider how we interact with others' and *'reaching in* to understand ourselves in relation to others' (The Learning Community, PYP Programme, 2018, page 13), educators become role models for their students by being calm, social and respectful leaders. Based on the IB foundational principle of international-mindedness, educators are encouraged to reach beyond the boundaries of their own school to connect with colleagues further afield. Making connections with other like-minded educators with shared IB values from around the world nurtures our own sense of community and wellbeing.

By taking care of ourselves – socially and emotionally – we can authentically lead by example. In this handbook, I aim to share the recipe for creating a calm and collaborative classroom filled with happy, high-achieving students and educators!

About Quirky Kid

The first Quirky Kid Clinic was founded in 2007 in Sydney, Australia by Dr Kimberley O'Brien and Leonardo Rocker.

Quirky Kid® has since evolved into an Educational Publisher of award-winning programs like Basecamp®, Power Up and The Best of Friends® Program, used in classrooms and clinics around the world. Quirky Kid is recognized for creativity, innovation and more than two decades of experience in educational psychology.

About the author

Kimberley provides consultancy to parents, school leaders and brands such as Lego®, Pilot Pen® and Cartoon Network® on child development and student wellbeing.

Her PhD research (Monash) on Belonging, Loneliness, Self Esteem and Friendship Quality Among Students in Transition from Primary to Secondary School, led Kimberley to author the award-winning Best of Friends® program for children aged 7 to 12 years: bof.quirkykid.com.au.

As the host of Impressive, a podcast for parents and educators, Kimberley tackles topics based on the clinical issues arising at Quirky Kid. She also plays an active role in the media with her knack for solving problems from the child's perspective.

According to Kimberley, her two greatest achievements include travelling solo across Africa, and giving birth to her son, Ben, in the family station wagon.

CHAPTER 1

The importance of wellbeing and SEL

> **IN A NUTSHELL**
> - This chapter introduces and defines the concept of wellbeing. Wellbeing is now understood as an individual state but also as being symbiotic to class and whole-school wellbeing. Strategies are suggested for whole-school and classroom wellbeing.
> - Social and emotional wellbeing is an important aspect of general wellbeing and is core to the IB framework. In the classroom, social and emotional learning (SEL) can occur through teacher modelling; strategies for introducing modelling behaviour to the classroom are suggested.
> - This chapter includes a checklist to implement wellbeing in a whole school or a single classroom, depending on the support of school leaders.
> - Specific strategies are also provided to give students roles and responsibilities as part of the wellbeing movement.
> - Wellbeing in the classroom cannot occur without organization. This chapter includes how to plan wellbeing initiatives into the schedule for best results.

Introduction

'They may forget what you said, but they will not forget how you made them feel.'
Carl W Buehner

Children are more sensitive than adults, given that their senses of smell, hearing, sight, taste and touch are heightened in comparison to their parents and teachers. Students are more likely to be distracted by the hum of a ceiling fan and more likely to be upset by a raised voice or sudden movement than a colleague in the staff room. A child's ability to recover from an unexpected event is also likely to take longer than it would for an adult with more life experience.

In most contexts, children typically have less control over their environment compared to the adults in the room. Teachers, for example, monitor the temperature of the room, the volume of the voices, the sequence and amount of time invested in each activity. For children, a subtle change in an adult's demeanour, or an abrupt request to change from one activity to the next, can trigger an unintended emotional response.

This chapter explores the importance of wellbeing and SEL in the Primary Years Programme (PYP) classroom.

Wellbeing in the PYP classroom

The term *wellbeing* is defined as 'the state of being comfortable, happy and healthy' (www.lexico.com/definition/well-being). There is a well-established link between physical activity and psychological wellbeing, indicating that

Chapter 1 The importance of wellbeing and SEL

individuals who engage in regular exercise experience more positive emotions (Malcolm *et al.*, 2013). Oxytocin is a neurotransmitter released in response to positive events in our environment, such as physical or social activity. On any given school day, activity breaks which include opportunities to socialize will boost both teacher and student wellbeing.

■ The teacher's wellbeing

Teacher wellbeing directly impacts student wellbeing. By understanding how our own wellbeing influences the children in our care, we develop greater self-awareness and an unwavering commitment to the importance of wellbeing as a foundation for learning. According to Chief Executive Sinéad McBrearty of UK's Education Support, 'Good teaching requires the highest levels of physical, social and emotional energy.' This was echoed in the results of the Teacher Wellbeing Index 2019, which revealed work-related stress in the teaching profession has increased for the third year in a row, with sharp rises in tearfulness, insomnia and irritability among teachers.

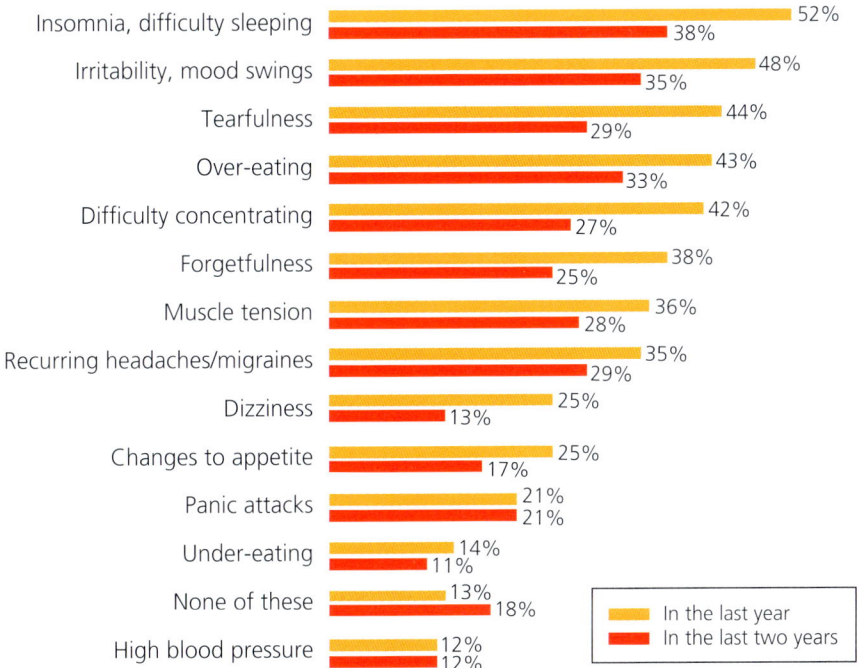

2019 Base: All education professionals, in the last year (n = 2 731); in the last two years (n = 2 154)

Note: A reflective question, asking respondents in 2019 for their perceptions relating to both 2019 and 2018

Symptoms experienced by education professionals in the last 1–2 years.
Source: www.educationsupport.org.uk/sites/default/files/teacher_wellbeing_index_2019.pdf

■ The classroom environment

The environment in which we live, work or study also influences our physical, social and emotional wellbeing. By developing a shared understanding of health and wellbeing across the entire IB learning community, students and teachers stand to benefit. A PYP classroom filled with fresh air, pockets of sunlight, a cosy reading corner, handmade art and plant life is likely to feel very nurturing and safe for students. The calm voice of a caring teacher will also influence the atmosphere. Comfortable, breathable clothes and soft footwear allow adults to move gently and quietly in the classroom. This helps students to relax and absorb more information. In my opinion, the 'clip-clop' of high heels on hard floors can distract and intimidate children.

As students mature, their needs change in terms of their learning environment and what they need to feel safe. Early adolescents will readily engage with educators only after trust has been established. Being clear on the rules of the Middle Years Programme (MYP) as students transition from the PYP is a good place to start. Research suggests early adolescents are more likely to victimize same-aged peers post-transition, for example, from PYP to MYP (Dempsey *et al.*, 2009; Heaven *et al.*, 2008; Pellegrini and Long, 2002). Educators can best support MYP students with increased supervision.

The theme of ensuring student safety in order to provide a nurturing learning environment continues as students enter the Diploma Programme (DP). As global citizens, students of the DP study beyond the classroom and need educators to recommend the best sources for research, to ensure their safety in the online community and the quality of their work. This structure, along with more regular communication between educators and individual students, ensures that learners feel safe and nurtured.

■ The role of school leaders

School leaders who nurture the wellbeing of teachers also ensure a greater sense of wellbeing among students (Durlak *et al.*, 2015; Roffey, 2019; Weissberg, 2019). Creating a shared vision for teacher wellbeing may include setting limits to ensure a manageable workload, encouraging healthy behaviours and providing initiatives to strengthen social networks, such as mentoring programs and professional development at lunchtime gatherings.

Anyone who has accessed quality content can appreciate the extra energy and enthusiasm cognitive stimulation brings. When educators take this back to the classroom, every student benefits. Being nurtured in a well-resourced workplace of any kind has the same outcome. Clients or customers are given more time, attention, support and respect. Students receive this same boost to their wellbeing when we invest in our educators.

■ Effective teamwork and collaboration

Effective teamwork and collaboration underpins teaching in all IB programmes (IBO, 2017). This refers to the collaborative relationship between teachers and students, but also includes promoting teamwork and collaboration between students. A focus on teamwork in the classroom can be challenging for students as they develop turn-taking, listening and negotiation skills. As such, teachers become practised at modelling problem-solving skills and emotional regulation to help students develop greater resilience within the learning community.

■ Generating support for wellbeing initiatives

One teacher can start the process and the momentum will build from the positive feedback your students will share with their parents and the observations of your colleagues. In my experience as a student wellbeing consultant, many schools decide to implement a whole-school wellbeing initiative in response to a traumatic event, such as a death within the student population. Alternatively, the decision to implement a wellbeing initiative may come from a forward-thinking principal or from a ground swell of parents or teachers with a commitment to prioritizing the social and emotional wellbeing of all students.

EDUCATOR'S CHECKLIST

How to generate support for wellbeing initiatives at your school

- ✔ Use your communication board or staff room to display wellbeing initiatives and related research.
- ✔ Organize for a wellbeing consultant to speak at a staff meeting or assembly.
- ✔ Gather a list of colleagues who are interested in joining a small and friendly wellbeing committee.
- ✔ With permission from the school leader, recruit students who would like to join Operation Wellbeing.
- ✔ Schedule a fun whole-school wellbeing initiative launch party with a guest speaker (or yourself) to introduce the idea and gather support.
- ✔ Think music, flowers, good vibes and warm connections – you and your wellbeing team can do this!

SEL in the PYP classroom

Social and emotional learning (SEL) is designed to boost the social and emotional wellbeing of students, resulting from strong social relationships and good psychological health (Cooker *et al.*, 2016). Social and emotional wellbeing is embedded within a culture of support, while SEL is part of the official and unofficial IB curriculum. This entails offering care for others and accepting care for oneself.

Research shows that academic achievement increases and is sustained when the social and emotional needs of students are prioritized (Mahoney *et al.*, 2018). Conversely, students who are exposed to prolonged academic pressure in countries such as China, Korea and Singapore are more prone to chronic stress, depression, anxiety and suicide ideation (Siu, 2019). New programs in China are trying to reduce the pressure on students by allowing outdoor exams.

An outdoor exam in China

New research suggests that students with greater social and emotional wellbeing are likely to perform an average of 13 percentile points higher academically than their non-SEL peers (Taylor *et al.*, 2017).

In practice, SEL begins as a part of a whole-school commitment to nurturing the social and emotional wellbeing of others and oneself. In the classroom, teachers should role model how to develop and maintain positive social relationships through greater self and social awareness.

> **HOW EDUCATORS CAN MODEL SELF-AWARENESS AND EMOTIONAL REGULATION**
>
> A teacher may feel excited about a new activity she has prepared for the class. She needs to use her laptop to access different types of music, but the laptop starts an automated update just as the students are waiting for the first song to begin. They wait patiently while she attempts to fix the problem but this takes longer than anticipated and she becomes impatient. This is an opportunity to turn to the students and say, 'I'm feeling really frustrated right now. I can feel myself rushing and worrying as I try to resolve this quickly, so I'll take a break and close the laptop until I feel calmer. We can do this later. Thanks for your patience, class, I really appreciate it.' The ability to articulate an emotion you are experiencing in the moment and to share a technique you are using to regulate this feeling is an example of self-awareness.

In a social context, teachers can model social awareness by pausing and considering different points of view. By taking the opportunity to see at least two sides to every story, teachers will help students to empathize with others and to better understand the reasons for their feelings.

Teachers in PYP classrooms are encouraged to practise SEL techniques by modelling techniques to stay calm, such as opening a window, taking a deep breath, drinking water and expressing feelings of frustration as they arise in a calm voice. Social issues between students are normalized and resolved by listening and turn-taking to understand the different perspectives. Encouraging students to consider another point of view and to model the use of empathy is helpful as these young people discover SEL.

The benefits of wellbeing and SEL

Over time, students exposed to SEL become more attuned to peer dynamics and more able to express themselves, develop friendships, negotiate and/or resolve conflict. This attitude is soon reflected in the broader school community and can be easily absorbed by visitors to the school. A whole-school approach to SEL ensures students are exposed to consistent role models and a safe environment to practise SEL principles. By enabling students to be part of a community committed to valuing social and emotional wellbeing, skills such as emotional regulation are more easily adopted by observing adults who value this practice.

Wellbeing for the IB PYP: Teaching for Success

Strategies for implementing wellbeing

■ For the classroom

Encourage students to pick flowers and display these in jars in the classroom

Bring elements of nature into the classroom, such as hanging up a decorated tree branch

Start small – a single flower in a glass bottle or jar, a few drops of lavender oil on the cushions in your reading corner or gentle background music. Incorporate the outdoors – collect organic objects like seeds from a tree, use string to hang up an interesting tree branch, take your class outdoors for a barefoot walk on the grass. Or just open a window, take a stretch and tell the class how you are feeling! This is how we model emotional regulation to children.

By adding some elements of nature to the learning space, we are valuing our humanity, just as zoo keepers who bring fresh grass to animals in a man-made enclosure are building a close relationship with those in their care. Implementing wellbeing is about being more humane to ourselves and others. Humans need time and space to reconnect with their environment throughout the day. Encouraging students to take a stretch in the sun, to go barefoot or to pick some flowers for your glass jars will increase their capacity to focus in the afternoon.

Cognitive stimulation is also an important aspect of wellbeing – research has shown that prisoners in solitary confinement report a feeling of euphoria when given a milk carton to study after months without reading material. Imagine a very long bus or plane trip without entertainment. I felt energized after visiting a classroom with very detailed and interesting information about a diverse range of projects displayed in each student's 'station' (or cubicle), compared to the feeling of lethargy after leaving a preschool with toddlers running in circles in an indoor space. Student and teacher wellbeing starts with the learning environment, and is closely followed by the relationships fostered in these spaces.

CASE STUDY

How one educator started a whole-school wellbeing initiative

Vicky was excited to join the team at a large urban primary school. Based in an area of disadvantage, student enrolments had declined after the recent closure of the local steelworks as many families relocated due to high unemployment in the suburbs surrounding the school.

In her first month of teaching, Vicky and her colleagues experienced a change in their school's leadership team, and 11 out of 47 staff members were made redundant. There was low morale among the educators and Vicky began to consider teaching overseas, until she realized how much she could do in the current circumstances.

She couldn't help but give stability to the students in her class. They wanted to know her and seemed to crave the commitment she brought when she first moved to the area. Vicky saw opportunities everywhere to bring hope in the face of financial stress. She decided to see if small changes could make a big social and emotional impact on her students and colleagues.

With the permission of the new leadership team, Vicky invited all the members of the school staff to be part of the 'school wellbeing team', to counteract the current climate with positive whole-school initiatives for students and staff. She made a few colourful flyers and pinned three around the school – one in the admin area, one in the staff kitchen and one inside the staff toilet. The next day Vicky was approached by many individuals who praised her idea and offered to help, or confirmed they would come to the meeting.

On the morning of the first gathering, Vicky was nervous. She was worried nobody would support her idea or that people might think she was 'too new' with 'no right to change things'. To combat her nerves, Vicky opened all the windows in the staff room to freshen the air, put on some background music and filled some small jars with water for the tiny flowers she found in the garden outside. Finally, Vicky pulled out a brief wellbeing survey she had created. She wanted to know what they could offer to foster wellbeing. Her initiative was about starting a groundswell, not hosting a one-woman show.

Vicky warmly greeted each person as they entered the room. She was pleased to see the school gardener, an admin assistant and four teachers, including two from the leadership team. They all seemed genuinely happy to trial something new without a budget and thanked Vicky for having the courage to put up the flyers. Vicky was humbled and pleased to be supported by her more experienced colleagues – this was going to be fun!

In that first meeting, they sketched out a draft wellbeing program, including making better use of garden space, allowing more background music and organizing social events for the whole-school community. Afterwards, Vicky sent a group email to all school staff and parents to share the outcome of the meeting and a link to the wellbeing survey she had created. It asked: 'What makes you feel good about our school?' and 'What would you like to do to make it even better?' She asked them to rate their sense of wellbeing at school on a scale of 1 to 10.

Monthly meet-ups ensued, vegetables from the garden were sold at the school gate and a musical dad wrote a new, upbeat school song. There was a thank you breakfast for the school gardener and a new chicken coop was built by the senior students. New roles and responsibilities encapsulated the student population, with most students earning their 'Wheelbarrow Licence' and 'Certificate in Egg Gathering'.

A pre- and post-wellbeing survey comparison of educators' responses revealed an 80% increase in wellbeing over a 12-month period based on self-ratings. Of the 451 students, parents and school staff, 76% felt more engaged at school and 92% of the school community had developed friendships within the school. Vicky published the 2019 wellbeing survey results in the school newsletter, along with photos of their whole-school breakfast, complete with fresh eggs, happy faces, healthier children and herbs from the garden.

■ Classroom participation and wellbeing

Students need to feel encouraged and safe to raise their hand in class

To raise your hand in a large group takes courage. To risk failure by taking a guess is even more commendable. Setting some ground rules, such as, 'No put downs', including snickers or negative noises or name-calling, is a great place

to start. Enforcing that rule with consistent reminders for those who forget will ensure greater classroom participation. Feeling safe is an essential part of social and emotional wellbeing.

Wellbeing can also be implemented by creating a long list of exciting roles and responsibilities for your students to share. A special or important task gives students structure and status. It could be wearing headphones and doing 'tech support' at assemblies, raising the school flag, turning on the light and opening the windows each morning, taking fruit scraps to a worm farm or jumping on cardboard for recycling. Special jobs create a sense of belonging, and this fosters student wellbeing in the school community.

■ Wellbeing in student–teacher relations

There is nothing more important than the relationship between a student and their teacher when it comes to school engagement. Making a positive start requires the use of a calm and gentle voice tone and passive body language – try crouching down and positioning yourself side-by-side (rather than face-to-face) in your one-to-one conversations with students. Sustained eye contact can be difficult for students who lack confidence with adults, but your voice and consistently calm demeanour will form the basis of a trusting relationship.

Unfortunately, some students and their parents can have preconceived ideas about teachers, and negative perceptions may be difficult to change. Be reassured that it is not your job to win over every parent, but children are more likely to be swayed by praise and positive experiences. Yelling and deliberately humiliating students in front of their peers can have a long-lasting impact on the teacher–student relationship, but a heart-felt apology is one way to take responsibility.

Planning is an essential step in managing stress in reaction to everyday triggers. Turning on some quiet music is a better way to settle a rowdy class than a raised voice. Non-verbal cues, like the teacher's raised hand or a clapping sequence, will attract the attention of a crowd. Rewarding the desired behaviour or capturing the moment with a photo to later print and display will also create a focus on what the class has achieved.

■ Scheduling wellbeing activities

A wellbeing activity, such as a walk on the grass, may take place in the morning as a type of early intervention to avoid social and emotional issues arising later in the day, such as frustration or agitation. Engaging the senses at different times throughout the day with background music in a tactile art lesson, or a chance to lie on scented pillows in the reading corner will reduce any rising frustrations or agitation between peers. Observe the reactions of your students, and this will help you to know when to schedule wellbeing activities the following day. Monitoring your own wellbeing will also guide this process. If you need outdoor time in the afternoon, schedule your barefoot walk after lunch to ensure your leadership is calm and charismatic.

Outdoor time should be scheduled when both the students and you, as the teacher, need it most

Useful resources

The following resources are designed to enhance students' social and emotional learning and overall wellbeing in the PYP classroom:

- National Children's Bureau, 'A whole school framework for emotional well-being and mental health': **www.ncb.org.uk/sites/default/files/field/attachment/NCB%20School%20Well%20Being%20Framework%20Leaders%20Resources%20FINAL.pdf**
- 'Your Emotions' series by Brian Moses (Wayland, 1993): **www.hachettechildrens.co.uk/titles/brian-moses/your-emotions-i-feel-sad/9781526305206/**

- 'Feelings and Emotions' series by Brian Moses and Kay Barnham (Wayland, 2017): **http://www.hachettechildrens.co.uk/titles/mike-gordon/feelings-and-emotions-feeling-sad/9781526300720/**
- *The Hurt* by Teddi Doleski (Paulist Press, 1983)
- *How to Be a Friend* by Laurie Krasny Brown (Little, Brown Books for Young Readers, 1998)
- PYP Friends series: *A New Friend, Ups and Downs, Fair Play, Lochie's Little Lie* and *The Sleepover* (Hodder Education, 2020)
- PYP ATL Skills Workbook series: *Growth Mindset: Self-Motivation, Perseverance and Resilience; Interpersonal Relationships; Mindfulness;* and *Social and Emotional Intelligence and Emotional Management* (Hodder Education, 2020)
- This video highlights the necessity of SEL in the IB continuum for sustained academic achievement: **vimeopro.com/iboorg/the-ib-continuum/video/150154575**

CHAPTER 2
Wellbeing and the Learner Profile

> **IN A NUTSHELL**
> - This chapter introduces and discusses the 10 learning behaviours at the heart of the PYP that can be utilized to encourage student wellbeing.
> - Each of these learning behaviours can be encouraged in different ways by conscious teacher leadership.
> - Each learning behaviour description is accompanied by detailed exercises to implement or inspire.

The IB Learner Profile includes 10 learning behaviours at the heart of the PYP. Each of these can be encouraged through activities designed to boost student wellbeing along with the specific learning behaviour. Through conscious leadership in the classroom, teachers can deliver beyond academic achievement, to include an overarching protective layer of student wellbeing to increase the fertility of the school community.

The learning behaviours or Learner Profile are commonly displayed in IB schools – along a pathway or in a garden for everyone to see. For teachers to encourage these attributes in students, a clear understanding of the characteristics related to each word is necessary. The following overview of the IB Learner Profile provides a foundation for the activities aligned with each attribute in this chapter.

Overview of the IB Learner Profile

Learning behaviour	Symbol	Characteristic
Inquirers		We nurture our curiosity, developing skills for inquiry and research. We know how to learn independently and with others. We learn with enthusiasm and sustain our love of learning throughout life.
Knowledgeable		We develop and use conceptual understanding, exploring knowledge across a range of disciplines. We engage with issues and ideas that have local and global significance.
Thinkers		We use critical and creative thinking skills to analyse and take responsible action on complex problems. We exercise initiative in making reasoned, ethical decisions.
Communicators		We express ourselves confidently and creatively in more than one language and in many ways. We collaborate effectively, listening carefully to the perspective of other individuals and groups.
Principled		We act with integrity and honesty, with a strong sense of fairness and justice, and with respect for the dignity and rights of people everywhere. We take responsibility for our actions and their consequences.
Open-minded		We critically appreciate our own cultures and personal histories, as well as the values and traditions of others. We seek and evaluate a range of points of view, and we are willing to grow from the experience.
Caring		We show empathy, compassion and respect. We have a commitment to service, and we act to make a positive difference in the lives of others and in the world around us.
Risk-takers		We approach uncertainty with forethought and determination; we work independently and cooperatively to explore new ideas and innovative strategies. We are resourceful and resilient in the face of challenges and change.
Balanced		We understand the importance of balancing different aspects of our lives – intellectual, physical, and emotional – to achieve wellbeing for ourselves and others. We recognize our interdependence with other people and with the world in which we live.
Reflective		We thoughtfully consider the world and our own ideas and experience. We work to understand our strengths and weaknesses in order to support our learning and personal development.

Practical strategies to foster wellbeing and learning behaviours

How do we encourage students to become 'Inquirers' without increasing academic pressure? And what if the concept of being a 'Risk-taker' triggers anxiety in students? Teachers need to ensure their students put each IB learning behaviour into action without impacting their emotional wellbeing.

The activities in this chapter are designed to draw out the existing Learner Profile characteristics from within the student audience and to build on these. As students develop an awareness of their own strengths and weaknesses in terms of the IB Learner Profile, they are more able to play to the strengths.

For example, a student who understands the love of asking questions and verbal communication is likely to identify with being an Inquirer and a Communicator. They may select projects based on their strengths to gain better results. Conversely, certain attributes, such as Principled, may feel like a weakness or an unexplored attribute waiting to be developed.

Educators may wish to reflect on the IB attributes on a daily basis, with questions like, 'Who worked on their ability to be Open-minded today, and how?' or they may wish to choose an 'Attribute of the week' to explore new ways of strengthening and displaying this aspect of the IB Learner Profile, allowing students to strengthen each of these attributes step by step.

From the very first lesson about the attributes, students will respond to a clear and concise definition, a child-friendly example and opportunities to practise the new skill or attribute in the classroom, the playground and the community. Revisiting each attribute on a regular basis will cement the concept. Students will develop a personal connection to some attributes very quickly, and others will require more time and attention.

When students have the opportunity to use the IB Learner Profile in a sentence and to practise each attribute across different contexts, their depth of understanding will continue to evolve, along with their appreciation of the word and how it applies to them personally. This process will enhance each student's self-awareness and their motivation to be more 'Reflective', 'Balanced' or 'Knowledgeable'.

In this section, each attribute is listed along with a variety of activities for teachers to share with their students. You can find these activities as photocopiable worksheets at the back of the book.

■ Inquirers

Have you ever questioned a choice you made? Revisited a decision, or thought about what you could have done differently? That's good! Asking yourself and those around you questions is healthy. Considering your options and making informed decisions builds confidence and is likely to trigger more questions, ideas and topics to research.

Educators and parents who are curious themselves are more likely to foster curiosity in children. By remaining conscious of the important role adults play as nurturers of inquiry, we are more likely to value the childlike quality of curiosity throughout our lives. Without this commitment to learning new things at every opportunity, children in our care would be at risk of becoming equally passive, uninspired to ask questions and limited by their role models.

Babies are born with an instinct for inquiry. A 1964 study found that infants as young as two months old showed a preference for unfamiliar patterns, suggesting new information is more appealing than content babies have seen before (Fantz, 1964). In 2007, a study recorded interactions between toddlers and their carers to reveal that children asked an average of 100 questions per hour and two-thirds of these were designed to elicit information (Chouinard, 2007).

■ How to inspire curiosity, independence and a love of lifelong learning

Nurturing children's curiosity requires parents and educators to feed their thirst for knowledge with more than just answers. We need to encourage their independence as Inquirers and praise their efforts to find answers to their questions. This starts by encouraging children to ask more questions and being motivated to find answers together. This provides an opportunity to role model a love of lifelong learning on an endless quest to inquire.

As the Nobel Prize-winning physicist Isidor Rabi explained when he collected his award, 'Every other mother in Brooklyn would ask her child after school: So? Did you learn anything today? But not my mother. "Izzy," she would say, "Did you ask a good question today?" That difference – asking good questions – made me a better scientist' (Rabi, 1960).

Thinking like an Inquirer

The following activity is designed to foster inquiry, inspire curiosity, trigger more questions and assemble new knowledge.

Step 1: Hold up a match box and ask your class to focus on the size of the box. You may wish to measure it and display the dimensions.

Step 2: Ask your class to go on a scavenger hunt to find five tiny items in the playground that will all fit in the box at the same time (think: seeds, stones or other interesting items).

Step 3: After returning to the classroom, ask the students to carefully line up all of their found items on their desk. Use magnifying glasses, if available, to closely study each item.

Step 4: Ask the students to choose one item and to then create a story about it, or draw it.

Step 5: Ask the class to walk carefully around the classroom and study all the items, slowly and closely, to be sure no items are lost, creating a sense of value and intrigue with everyday objects in familiar places.

■ Resource to foster inquiry

Smith, K. 2015. *Adventure Lab (Boxed Set): The Imaginary World of …, How to Be an Explorer of the World and Finish This Book*. New York. Penguin Books.

■ Knowledgeable

Psychologists are trained to use cognitive tests to determine a person's intelligence quotient (IQ). Children can have their IQ assessed in early childhood as the required tasks are mostly visual puzzles and timed tasks. David Wechsler, the creator of the world's most widely used intelligence test for children (Wechsler Intelligence Scales for Children), purposely excluded maths tasks and spelling lists to eliminate the influence of education on the results. The IQ test is designed to measure a child's natural-born intelligence, whether they have attended school or not.

Knowledge is factual information or skills acquired through experience or lessons learnt. Children who attend school have the advantage of gaining knowledge through experience *and* education. Educators are trained to engage with issues and ideas with local and global significance across a range of disciplines. Their guidance allows students to think more broadly about a topic and to consider all the factors involved.

From birth, children are actively participating, experimenting and observing peers and adults to acquire new skills. At school, knowledge is extended by encouraging children to test new skills in the classroom, and to gain competence and a sense of accomplishment, before applying the same principles in the community – locally and internationally.

Knowledgeable children typically have high self-esteem and are willing participants in class discussions. Others have the answers but may doubt themselves. Educators can protect the self-esteem of students with less knowledge by teaching research skills and the gathering of information before engaging in class discussions, in order to foster greater participation and confidence in the classroom.

Build your student's confidence by boosting their knowledge of the topic before a class discussion

■ How to engage with issues and ideas across a range of disciplines that have local and global significance

Applying an issue or idea to a range of disciplines – such as water absorption rates in science experiments, and asking students to write a story about water restrictions, for example, as a creative writing task – will facilitate a greater depth of understanding and allow children to apply their knowledge in different ways.

The following activity is designed to engage students with an issue or idea of local and global significance.

Step 1: Ask students to choose a topic, such as water use, recycling, animal rights, transport or food. The topic needs to be of relevance to your students and it also needs to be relevant to students of a similar age in a different part of the world. For example, fishing may be relevant to students in Alaska and in Sri Lanka for different reasons.

Step 2: Students should draw something from their local area that is related to their chosen topic. For example, if they chose food, they could draw what they eat at home.

Step 3: Students should then choose another part of the world as a different context in which to research their topic. For example, with food, they could draw popular dishes or foods from their chosen region, and place the picture on a map. This is an opportunity for students to practise research skills and to place images on a map, before sharing their findings in a class discussion.

Step 4: Ask the students to discuss these questions in groups:
- What do students around the world have in common?
- What differences did you discover in regard to your topic?
- What other questions did your research raise?

Discover the answers to your questions.

Share your new knowledge with your classmates.

■ Thinkers

We all feel frustrated when problems arise. Have you ever walked around an unfamiliar city when your phone is almost out of charge? Finding a shopkeeper who is willing to share a phone charger makes you feel like a problem-solver; a thinker; a genius! This is due to the dopamine reward rush triggered by problem-solving, also known as the 'Aha! moment' (Kounios and Beeman, 2009).

Children are natural problem-solvers. Most toddlers like to open cupboards, empty the contents and pull apart or taste any items of interest. Adults may feel tempted to give children solutions, but this only creates dependence and should be avoided. A problem-solver is a great asset to the classroom and the community. Giving children roles and responsibilities, such as raising the school flag or turning on the technology, will also enhance their capacity to work independently and overcome challenges.

With a growth mindset, students can develop skills and knowledge through effort, practice and persistence (Dweck, 2006). Educators can encourage students to tackle complex problems because our abilities can be improved upon with effort and the right strategies. This knowledge equates to an instant reduction in frustration, as we gain confidence in our problem-solving capacity. So, instead of walking around with a flat phone battery, feeling lost, we think ahead and problem-solve before an issue arises.

Chapter 2 Wellbeing and the Learner Profile

■ How to find solutions to solve complex problems

Finding solutions to complex problems

Step 1: Ask your students, 'Have you ever noticed a problem that needs fixing? I bet you have plenty of ideas! Draw or write about the problem on your worksheet.'

Step 2: Ask your students to break the problem down into smaller pieces. This will help them to solve it in parts, one step at a time.

For example, a garbage bin that is overflowing may have three parts to it:

1 Too much garbage	2 No one to empty bin	3 Garbage blowing into a river or ocean

Step 3: Ask the students to draw or write about three different parts of the problem they discovered.

Can they find a solution for each small part of the problem? For example:

1 Too much garbage	2 No one to empty bin	3 Garbage blowing into a river or ocean
Solution: Reduce the amount of waste or add an extra bin.	Solution: Volunteer to empty the bin more frequently or find someone who can.	Solution: Put a lid on the garbage bin and pull the waste from the water.

■ Communicators

Have you ever sat silently in a discussion and wished you had the confidence to contribute? Effective communication skills allow people to have a voice and to have their ideas acknowledged. Children are at a disadvantage when adults use verbal communication to engage them. Talking may come easily for some, but there are many other ways to express thoughts and feelings.

Behavioural issues often arise when children cannot adequately express themselves using verbal communication. Lashing out physically or throwing an object may replace phrases like, 'I am frustrated and I need some space.' At other times, children may withdraw or disengage when verbal communication is too heavily relied upon by educators as a medium by which to exchange ideas. Children who lack confidence in their communication skills often thrive when given other mediums to help them express themselves, such as visual arts, voice recording software, creative writing or drama.

Play-based activities that use tactile mediums, such as sand play, also help children to express themselves. By first asking the young person to run their fingers through sand in a tray, and giving options, such as, 'Is it cold or warm?', 'Smooth or rough?', most are drawn to the texture of the sand. To learn more about the young person, I often invite them to create a scene in the sand about home or school using miniature people and animals to represent the characters in the story. Based on the work of Dr Eliana Gil (Christensen & Thorngren, 2000), the sand tray is spun around after the scene is complete to give the child an opportunity to look at their story from different perspectives, and to consider other points of view.

■ How to express ourselves, listen and collaborate with others

Is it easier to listen/talk to someone if they are facing towards you or away from you?

Step 1: Ask students to find a partner, move to an open space and sit back to back.

Step 2: Students should take turns to talk and listen for 30 seconds each. One person talks, the other listens, and then they should switch roles. Both students will have a turn to talk and listen.

Step 3: Students should then turn around and face each other and try the same thing again. This time the listener can see the talker's eyes, hands and facial expressions. Swap over after 30 seconds.

Step 4: Ask the students to answer these questions together:

- Was it easier for you to listen when you were facing away from each other or sitting face to face? Why do you think this was the case?
- Was it easier to talk when you were facing away from each other or sitting face to face? Why do you think this was the case?

Step 5: Take a vote and see how many students preferred facing away and how many preferred sitting face to face when communicating. Discuss the outcomes with your class.

Principled

Listening to great leaders should be inspiring. Principled leaders act with integrity, honesty and fairness. We can all be principled by respecting the dignity and rights of people everywhere, and by taking responsibility for our actions and the consequences of those actions (IBO, 2017). Giving students access to the voices of Greta Thunberg and Malala Yousafzai, for example, demonstrates how young people with strong principles have attracted a supportive global audience.

Similarly, students are drawn to educators with principles, particularly when their principles are displayed every day in the classroom. When educators refuse to let students *put down*, *humiliate* or *speak negatively about others*, they are modelling strong principles. In addition to this, educators who choose to represent the voices of those who are underrepresented in the school community are creating space for minorities. Giving power to the powerless to bring about fairness and justice for all is part of being a positive role model for students and future generations.

Students, too, can be role models for each other by striving for greatness and bringing out the best in themselves and others. Consistently treating others with respect is an important aspect of being principled. During many classroom observations, I have noticed how educators can change their voice tone depending on who they are speaking to. These inconsistencies are often

Wellbeing for the IB PYP: Teaching for Success

more evident to the students than to the educator themselves. For this reason, self-awareness is an important first step for everyone on the journey towards great leadership.

Educators who represent the voices of the underrepresented are creating space for minorities

■ How to practise integrity, fairness and justice

Step 1: Ask students to consider the phrase:

'Be the change you want to see in the world.'
Mahatma Gandhi

Step 2: Students should imagine they have been selected to lead their country. As a leader with a strong sense of fairness, what changes would they like to implement? Ask them to make a list and to think about how these changes might affect the rights of people everywhere.

Step 3: How would students put these changes into practice? Ask them to write about, or draw a picture showing how they could be the change they want to see in the world.

■ Open-minded

To be open-minded is to embrace ideas that are different from your own, and to appreciate the concept, even if you disagree with it. Being interested in learning about different cultures, traditions and values for the sake of understanding an equally important viewpoint makes a person well-informed. A closed-minded person may challenge ideas that differ from their own, or they may resist opportunities to learn new ways of interpreting the same information.

Chapter 2 Wellbeing and the Learner Profile

Children interpret the value of another person by observing the adults in their life. If a parent shuts down a diverse point of view, or avoids a particular demographic, children learn to do the same. At school, students may feel conflicted when educators are open-minded about topics their parents may be less inclined to discuss. Exploring different viewpoints is part of being an open-minded educator in every internationally-minded IB classroom. This allows children to be more informed and to value the benefits of an open mind.

Research shows that children can shift their opinions and the influence of their parents through education and the friendships they form. For example, having friends of different races as a toddler and beyond reduces racism and increases intergroup warmth (Barlow *et al.*, 2009). Furthermore, educators who intentionally affirmed children's racial identities as part of the curriculum reported increases in students' learning across many domains of development (Ladson-Billings, 2009; Wright *et al.*, 2015).

■ How to seek, evaluate and appreciate different points of view

Appreciating different points of view

Step 1: Ask students to design a survey and gather different perspectives from other students at your school. Students should choose a topic which is likely to stimulate different points of view, and they should use a Likert scale for each question, such as the one shown on the next page.

Strongly disagree	Disagree	Undecided	Agree	Strongly agree
1	2	3	4	5

Step 2: Encourage your students to survey as many other students as possible within a set time period.

Step 3: Ask students to identify the one question in their survey with the most diverse range of responses, ie a mix of 5s and 1s.

Step 4: Ask students to consider the different points of view on this particular question. Why were the responses so diverse? Students should share their ideas with the class.

■ Caring

Educators can influence the amount of empathy, compassion and respect students show for themselves and others in the classroom, even if they cannot change a student's circumstances at home. Without strong and consistent leadership, social issues in a community can infiltrate the boundaries of a school. One school principal I spoke to led a team of committed educators who turned around a school's reputation after a stolen car was driven into the playground and set alight. It sounds like an extreme case, but when students are at risk in their communities, educators are often the most influential and life-changing role models.

Teaching empathy, compassion and respect starts with an emotional investment in each individual student and the time required to foster a connection. This will vary depending on the student and their own personal circumstances. Trust is a key component in any teacher–student relationship. As an educator, you will influence young people, even if they keep their distance. Your actions will be observed by those around you, and being consistently caring will help others to learn how to apply empathy, compassion and respect.

Many schools offer their students the opportunity to raise awareness for a cause, such as youth homelessness, animal cruelty or the impact of climate change on humanity. Educators can also share their own experiences of volunteering, at a soup kitchen, for example, or they can use YouTube to show students how 'random acts of kindness', or opportunities to 'pay-it-forward' are happening in our society (www.youtube.com/watch?v=GdYJr03eJjE). This shifts a student's focus from their own situation, and allows them to consider how they can positively impact the world with empathy, compassion and respect for others.

Chapter 2 Wellbeing and the Learner Profile

Building empathy, compassion and respect

■ **How to build empathy, compassion and respect**

Step 1: Ask students to list ideas that would be helpful to, or appreciated by others.

Step 2: Create a marble jar in your classroom to reward random acts of kindness. (Note: a marble jar reward system involves placing an empty jar in a prominent position. When a student participates in a random act of kindness, a marble will go into the jar. Once the jar is full, students have reached their reward. Base the size of the jar depending on the reward or the needs of your class – a smaller jar could mean a smaller, simpler reward as it will be quicker to fill, while a large jar could mean a big reward.)

Step 3: Brainstorm a new list each week with a different focus. Start with your classroom and broaden your reach to include the playground, the staff room, the canteen and then move out into the community.

■ **Resources to teach empathy and compassion**

How to show empathy: www.wikihow.com/Show-Empathy

Old People's Home for 4 Year Olds: www.youtube.com/watch?v=13_rJVvxx_g

Find guest speakers from organizations supporting asylum seekers or the elderly in your community. Invite parents to attend to build empathy, compassion and respect within your school community.

■ Risk-takers

Children take risks in their play, such as balancing building blocks

Risk-taking allows humans to test their own boundaries to find out what they can and can't do. Risk-takers can appreciate the excitement of uncertainty. Children take risks in their play as part of learning. Balancing a block at the highest point of a tower may cause it to topple over, but if the tower stays in place, there is a sense of exhilaration. According to research, children who are risk-takers have better risk management skills, resilience and self-confidence (Brussoni et al., 2015).

No one learns without making mistakes (Guzman Ingram, 2017). Educators who reward perseverance in their students are acknowledging the challenges of failure and the energy required to push through uncertainty. Sharing your own mistakes and the failures of other role models on a regular basis can help students adopt terms such as 'the power of yet' – that is, 'I can't do it *yet*' as opposed to 'I can't do it'.

Normalizing mistakes and suggesting a 'retake', as though every failure is part of a movie that can be edited, empowers young people to get used to setbacks. Working towards a shared goal for the whole class, such as a Perseverance Party, gives educators an opportunity to highlight the effort and patience that learning requires. Giving students the responsibility of pushing outside their own comfort zones will ensure that students with perfectionist traits feel in control of their own incremental challenges.

■ How to foster resourceful, resilient risk-takers

Step 1: Explain the power of 'yet' – use the phrase 'I can't do this *yet*' rather than 'I can't do this'.

Step 2: Set your students a challenge that is slightly more difficult than their regular classwork.

Step 3: Listen to how your students respond. While some may say, 'This looks challenging', others may push the work aside and complain, 'This is too hard!' Record their responses for all to see.

Step 4: Set a timer for two minutes and ask students to engage with the material, to *persevere*. Reward sustained effort over time. Ask them to self-reflect on how they found the challenge and any barriers they encountered while trying to persevere.

Step 5: Set a daily or weekly challenge to encourage risk-taking using the timer to reward slight extensions in sustained effort. Ask students to rate their own risk-taking as learners during one set task:

✔ 40 = 'I can't do this *yet*'   ✔ 0 = 'I can't do this'

Ask students to make a graph of their own risk-taking based on their self-ratings at the end of the challenging set task. See the example below.

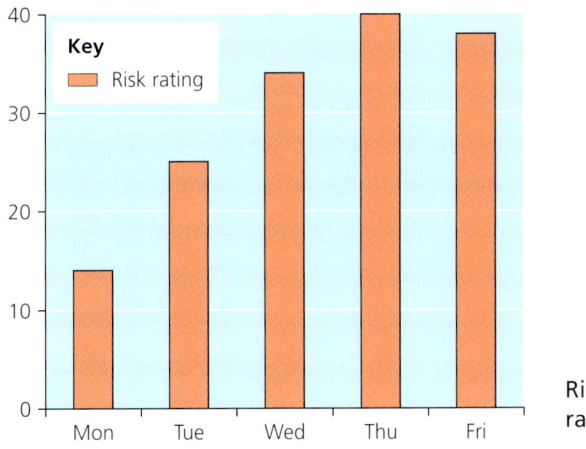

Risk-taker's self-rating – week 1

Step 6: Praise perseverance and being courageous enough to make mistakes. Host a Perseverance Party to celebrate your progress as a class.

■ Resource to foster perseverance

The power of believing that you can improve: www.ted.com/talks/carol_dweck_the_power_of_believing_that_you_can_improve/transcript?language=en#t-324080

■ Balanced

Have you ever felt like you need to do more exercise? Maybe you have had times when you have felt more emotional and less inclined to socialize. Emotional connectivity remains a core part of being human (Cacioppo *et al.*, 2015). Finding balance will help, and teaching children how to achieve balance is the role of parents and educators.

Being balanced is about seeking out cognitive stimulation, selecting healthy food options, prioritizing social opportunities and scheduling daily exercise. Putting these values into practice throughout the life span is the key to maintaining physical and mental health.

Children are influenced by the choices made by the adults who care for them. Daily decisions around how much screen time a child is allowed, the types of food provided and a willingness to arrange social opportunities with school friends or neighbours all have a significant impact on a child's balance – socially, physically and emotionally. Children are more likely to adopt a balanced lifestyle when educators and parents promote similar values.

■ How to recognize our interdependence and our own social, emotional and physical needs

Step 1: Explain interdependence. Discuss your understanding of the word with a partner.

> *Interdependence* means individuals, communities and nations who can rely on each other. With interdependence, humans have different roles – farming the land, building houses, delivering products to supermarkets. One human needs to depend on another to make our society work. That is interdependence.

Chapter 2 Wellbeing and the Learner Profile

Step 2: Ask students to study the image below.

This is a family of hunters and gatherers. At night, the fire was a place to keep warm and listen to stories. By day, some hunted and others gathered food to survive. The children collected firewood, and helped to carry water and keep the babies safe

Ask students: Why do you think hunters and gatherers did not live alone? They should list three ideas.

Step 3: Ask students to study the image below.

SOCIETY

This is a modern community. There are many different jobs in today's human society, compared to the hunters and gatherers. There are teachers, firefighters, shop assistants – all kinds of jobs! In many households, children help to cook dinner, keep the house tidy and go to school

Ask students: Do you think we still need to live together in today's society? Why or why not?

Chapter 2 Wellbeing and the Learner Profile

Step 4: Ask students to study the image below.

This is an image of a woman who is dressed up and her hair is neat, suggesting she may be going to meet someone (socially). She is doing exercise by riding her scooter to take care of herself (physically) and her facial expression appears calm (emotionally). She appears *balanced* – socially, emotionally and physically

Step 5: Students should draw three circles (see diagram on the right) and write 'socially', 'emotionally' and 'physically' in each circle. They should think about their routine and draw or write, in each circle, what they do to keep themselves balanced and how they take care of themselves – socially, emotionally and physically.

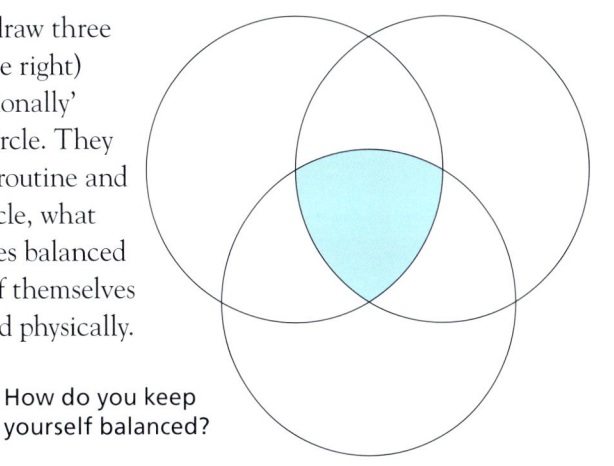

How do you keep yourself balanced?

35

Step 6: Ask students to share their ideas in small groups and to discuss the ideas below.

Socially	Physically	Emotionally
☑ Go to a playground	☑ Walk up stairs	☑ Hug yourself
☑ Invite a friend over	☑ Run home	☑ Pat an animal
☑ Share something	☑ Ride a bike	☑ Put flowers in a vase
☑ Post a surprise	☑ Join a team sport	☑ Get nice and clean
☑ Visit a neighbour	☑ Skip with a rope	☑ Take a big stretch
☑ Plan a little party	☑ Do sit-ups	☑ Write in a journal

How to take care of yourself

■ Reflective

To reflect is to think about what we have learned and what we can do with our new knowledge. Sometimes it can be difficult to think about what we have learned but it helps to think about the lesson or activity by drawing on all your senses, including what you saw, tasted, smelled and felt at the time of experiencing the new information.

Children are often asked to reflect on their weekend, or what they did in the holidays. It is easy to start with a list of events and then to dig deeper to better understand the lessons learnt. To be reflective, we must process the information and evaluate it. Being reflective is about considering our own strengths and weaknesses. This helps us to know where we need to improve and how we can better contribute in the future.

For example, children who love to learn facts will often memorize information and share it with others. Reciting the facts aloud helps them to process the data, while the responses they receive from others help them to evaluate this skill. Most people can listen to a few facts and may respond with, 'That's interesting', but after listening to a very long list of facts the response may be, 'Okay, that's enough now'.

Chapter 2 Wellbeing and the Learner Profile

Reflecting on these different responses with the child is an opportunity to consider what worked and what didn't. With reflection, the child might start to focus on reading social cues, such as a sigh or a fast nod, suggesting it is time to 'hurry up'. As an outcome of reflection, the child may set themselves a limit on how many facts to recite before asking the listener a question. Without reflection, lessons take longer to learn.

■ **How to thoughtfully consider the world, our own strengths and our weaknesses**

Step 1: Think about all the textures in the world around you. Give examples and allow students to touch soft, rough, jagged or fluffy textures found in your classroom.

Step 2: Encourage your students to explore the school grounds to seek out different textures. Ask them to collect a diverse range of samples of textures to stick in a journal.

Here is an example:

Photograph of journal item courtesy of Olivia Rocker (aged 12)

37

Wellbeing for the IB PYP: Teaching for Success

Step 3: Ask students to consider their own strengths and weaknesses as textures. Some parts of ourselves may be solid and strong. These are our strengths. Other parts may be soft and fragile. These are our weaknesses. Using the different textures found in the playground, ask students to craft a sculpture or symbol of themselves.

Give students two options:

a   Stick the textures in a journal in the form of yourself, labelling your own strengths and weaknesses.

b   Create a sculpture of yourself using the textures and write a sentence about how it is like you.

Here is an example:

'I am balanced most of the time, but if I tip over I'm still learning how to fix things myself.'

Creating a sculpture using different textures

Step 4: Reflect on this activity in a class discussion:
- How did it feel to collect the different textures? Discuss.
- How did it feel to consider your own strengths and weaknesses? Discuss.
- How did you feel about creating an image of yourself with the textures? Discuss.

■ **Recommended resources**
- Levy, J. 2012. *How to Be a World Explorer: Your All-Terrain Training Manual.* London. Lonely Planet Publications
- Smith, K. 2013. *The Pocket Scavenger.* London. Penguin Random House

CHAPTER 3

ATL skills

> ### IN A NUTSHELL
>
> - This chapter will introduce and discuss the research in relation to wellbeing among primary school students and the following three Approaches to Learning (ATL) skills:
>   - ☐ Social skills
>   - ☐ Communication skills
>   - ☐ Self-management skills
> - Children's social skills are discussed in terms of their importance for the individual and the benefits of peer relationships in classrooms and playgrounds.
> - Communication skills across the developmental continuum are explained, as well as how to boost communication skills using non-verbal cues in classrooms.
> - Self-management skills are discussed, including microskills, such as emotional regulation, recognizing triggers and praising progress.
>
> There are additional chapters in this book that provide activities for educators to implement, designed to develop the social and communication skills of students and their capacity to self-manage social and emotional triggers. The current chapter explores the role of educators in helping students to develop and practise these important skills.

Children's social skills and wellbeing

Loneliness and exclusion can undermine a child's wellbeing

There is evidence to suggest that the quality of a child's social skills and their subsequent wellbeing influence the physical health and competence of individuals throughout their life span (Barblett and Maloney, 2010; Gluckman, 2011). *Loneliness* is defined as an awareness of deficiencies in one's own social relationships and the associated sense of sadness and longing for friendships or social unions (Asher and Paquette, 2003). Interestingly, Walton and Cohen (2011) found a single instance of exclusion has the potential to undermine a child's wellbeing (Eisenberger *et al.*, 2003; Williams, 2009).

The literature suggests that children are very aware of deficiencies in their social relationships. By comparing themselves to other children at school who have greater social confidence, some young people experience a decline in self-esteem after starting school. As such, loneliness in childhood and adolescence is closely associated with social withdrawal (Rubin *et al.*, 2009) and feelings of victimization (Nishina *et al.*, 2005). Chronically lonely youth are more prone to psychological maladjustment and experience greater difficulty in engaging with others when new social opportunities arise.

Experiences of loneliness in childhood subsequently predict depressive symptoms in adolescence and adulthood (Fontaine *et al.*, 2009; Koenig *et al.*, 1994; Lasgaard *et al.*, 2011; Stegar and Kashdan, 2009; Witvliet *et al.*, 2010). This highlights the importance of detecting loneliness and social withdrawal early to prevent the onset of depressive symptoms in secondary school and to reduce the risk of chronic depression in adulthood.

Loneliness in childhood increases the risk of depressive symptoms in adolescence and beyond

■ Making friends

During primary school, the significance of making and keeping friends is well documented (Giannetti and Sagarese, 2001; Oberle *et al.*, 2011; Witvliet *et al.*, 2010). Belonging to a group invites more opportunities for preferential treatment between group members at the expense of non-group members (Hausmann *et al.*, 2009).

Gender differences in social skills are frequently reported in the friendship literature. Of particular interest are the findings that boys report fewer close friendships and greater difficulty resolving conflict. However, boys are more motivated to socialize with peers with similar activity-based interests and sporting talents, while girls are more drawn to intimacy in friendships, such as sharing personal information and making promises (Neilsen-Hewett, 2001).

Research has found gender differences in social skills and friendship choices

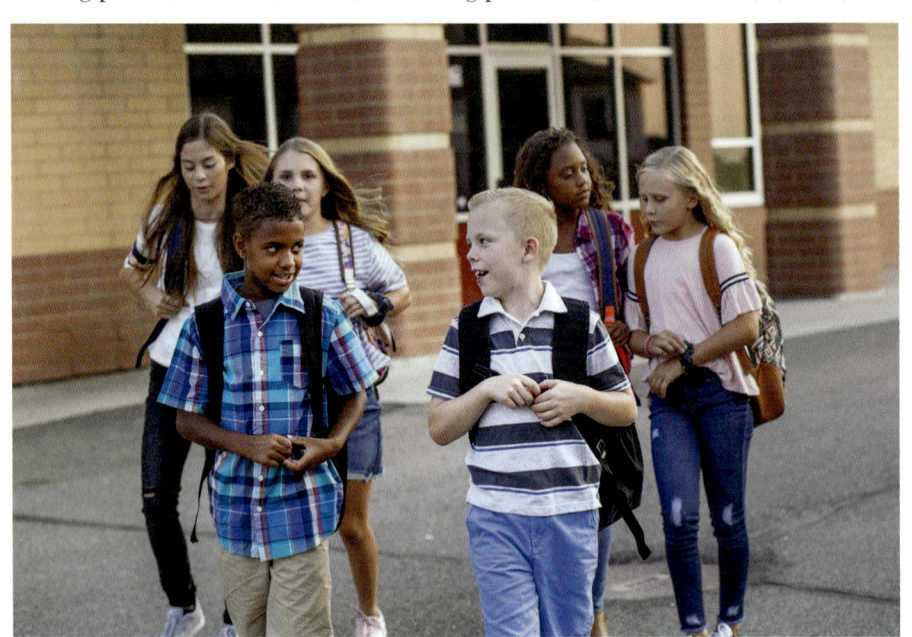

Children's communication skills and wellbeing

Most children love to talk to their parents and peers. Exchanging information about their shared interests or telling a story about something that happened often makes listening to a conversation between children either very specific and unrelatable or very amusing. At school, students are more likely to ask educators for clarification about the routine, and young students become good at guessing how their educator will respond to any given situation. By learning to read body language and to recognize any changes to their educator's voice tone, students begin to predict the flow of the day.

From infancy, babies learn how to communicate from watching their parents or primary carers. Facial expressions, playful utterances and differences in voice volume help to convey the emotion between parents and child.

Upon starting school, the positive influence of an educator cannot be underestimated as children develop more advanced communication skills. Educators who can listen carefully, express ideas logically, give and receive meaningful feedback, discuss a broad range of opinions clearly and negotiate respectfully make excellent role models for their students.

■ Communication and gender stereotypes

Communication is an important skill, with the potential to empower students worldwide. According to the literature, boys aged 11–13 years who report conflict within their friendships often lack the social and communication skills required to save the relationship, compared to same-aged girls, who resolve their issues with more frequent communication aimed at resolving the conflict (O'Brien, 2017).

There is ample research to indicate that boys and girls have different communication styles, even in primary school. Gender stereotypes extend to the possibility that boys may be socialized to limit intimacy within their friendships, in order to be considered masculine, while girls are encouraged to be nurturing by enquiring about the wellbeing of others, and these gender roles may be reinforced by their role models at home and school (Dornan, 2004). Traditional masculine norms include restricted emotions, avoidance of femininity, self-reliance, strength and aggression (Levant and Kopecky, 1995). Gender stereotypes have an influence on all of us – how we behave and how we relate to one another are influenced by our society's ideas and norms about gender.

In light of these influences, schools should be mindful that girls often receive more encouragement to offer friends help, care and guidance, while boys may not have had this experience. To remedy this, Chapter 5 is dedicated to practical strategies for educators to boost children's communication skills, regardless of gender.

Children's self-management skills and wellbeing

The concept of *self-management* refers to a person's capacity to independently cope with their own emotional responses triggered by any given situation and to persevere or push through adversity. As adults, we have become accustomed to absorbing new information and experiences with minimal outward emotional reaction – we may be feeling slightly different underneath the 'cool, calm and collected' exterior.

Teaching self-management to children is easier when we are able to articulate and share the details of this process. For example: 'I am listening to the new information, but I am also thinking, *oh no, how can I solve this problem without getting upset?*'

Children begin to learn to regulate their emotions from an early age

Learning to manage and respond to emotions in a healthy, positive way is a process children begin to refine from an early age. Psychologists call this *emotional regulation*. Parents and early childhood educators encourage toddlers to regulate their emotions by asking them to 'use your words'. In most cases, intermittent crying and tantrums decline when children learn to articulate their issues to adults or to solve problems themselves.

CHAPTER 4

ATL skills: Social skills

> **IN A NUTSHELL**
> - Children commonly experience conflict or confusion around social behaviours and friendships, and need assistance from adults to learn how to manage these.
> - Using case studies, this chapter offers activities to help children recognize their own behaviours and develop their social skills by:
>   - ☐ boosting empathy
>   - ☐ advocating for themselves and others
>   - ☐ mapping their feelings.
> - Each case study is accompanied by Dr Kimberley's Top 5 Tips for how to manage these common schoolyard or classroom situations.

This chapter provides educators with practical activities to teach children about social skills and the emotions we commonly experience when making and keeping friends. Each activity is designed to be visually engaging in order to simplify the complicated feelings and relationships that children often learn to navigate for the first time at school.

Children's friendships can be a source of stress for educators when young students lack the skills to effectively communicate and resolve issues as they arise. Stepping in to assist and model positive social skills is more helpful than suggesting children 'sort it out themselves', particularly for children under the age of eight years, who are usually open to learning new ways to resolve friendship issues.

To illustrate the situations most parents and professionals working with children are familiar with, this chapter includes three case studies to highlight the challenges students face as they learn to collaborate with others as their social and emotional intelligence develops.

Collaboration skills

The following case studies include a range of collaboration skills, including the ability to listen to others, show empathy, practise self-control and find solutions with resilience. Each case study has a practical activity relating to the issues exemplified in each student's story.

CASE STUDY

Jonas (7): Problems in the playground

Jonas loves the structure of the classroom, but in the playground he is overwhelmed by the noise, the activity and the lack of support. Jonas isn't clear on how to join a ball game and the rules seem to change depending on who is playing.

Jonas feels frustrated but he is not sure how to fix the situation. Everyone seems to be enjoying themselves, including the teacher on duty, but Jonas can't seem to relax.

The game is complicated and Jonas keeps making mistakes. When it is time to give another child a turn in the game, Jonas refuses. He yells, 'I'm not out!' and pushes the new player to the ground. Now Jonas is really in trouble.

How to help Jonas

1. Ask your class to create a video to explain the rules of the ball game to Jonas. This will promote discussion about the rules and highlight the inconsistencies. Show the video at a school assembly to explain the game to the whole school community.

2. Ask Jonas to choose the place he finds most relaxing in the playground. Encourage him to use this calm space to regulate his emotions and to avoid feeling overwhelmed. Praise Jonas for using the space.

3. Give Jonas more structure during breaks by providing a schedule, such as visiting the library on Monday, chess club on Tuesday, ball games on Wednesday, garden helper on Thursday and free play on Friday.

4. Introduce 'anger' as a topic for class discussion to normalize reactions to different triggers. Share your own triggers and how you manage anger – for example, by saying, 'I'm feeling tense, I'll open a window', or 'I'll make a cup of tea', or 'I'll come back to this when I'm calmer'. Ask the class to share their triggers and how they calm down. Role-play these ideas in small groups to give everyone a chance to practise a range of calming techniques.

5. Read these recommended children's books about anger management:
   - *I Feel Angry* by Brian Moses
   - *How to Take the Grrrrr out of Anger* by Elizabeth Verdick and Majorie Lisovskis

Chapter 4 ATL skills: Social skills

Discussing the topic of 'anger' in class helps to normalize reactions to different triggers

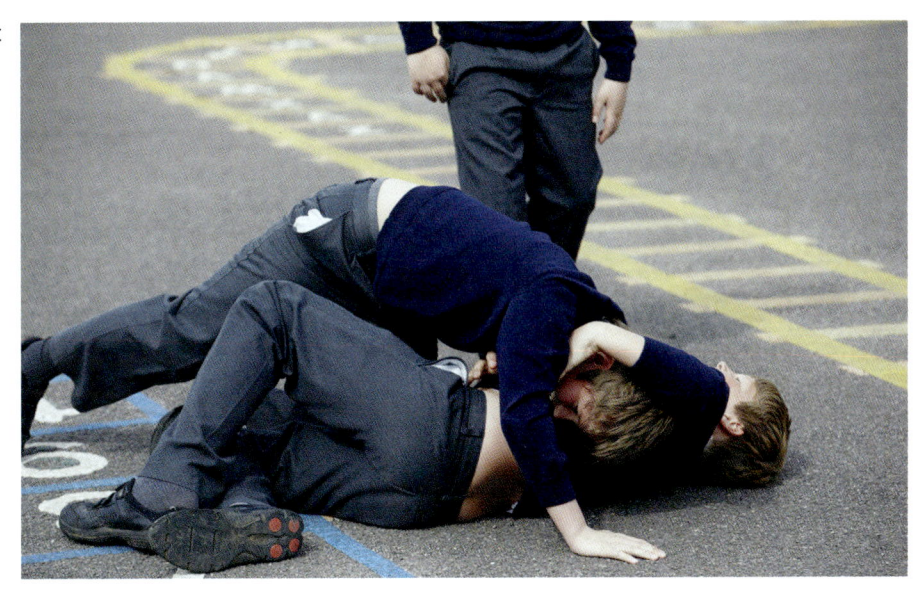

DR KIMBERLEY'S TOP 5 TIPS

To create a peaceful playground

1 Supervise closely and praise often.
2 Give more space when trust is established.
3 Give roles and responsibilities, such as handing out sports equipment, if more structure is required.
4 Ask students to create a video, explaining the agreed rules of a ball game to resolve conflict, if necessary.
5 Play music, plant a garden or create shade and spaces for quiet reading.

■ Activity 1: How to boost empathy with a mini playground scene

The purpose of this activity is to help students consider different perspectives and to increase empathy.

Encourage your students to think about an incident that has happened in their friendship group, or something they have experienced in the playground involving other students or teachers. It may be something they would like to change. This activity will help students to consider a different perspective and to literally see another point of view. Feel free to be creative and use the resources you have in or around your classroom.

Here is an example of a mini playground scene made from leaves and tree bark:

This concept of nature-based social and emotional learning (SEL) was developed by Dr Kimberley O'Brien

Here is a mini playground scene using paper to create the characters:

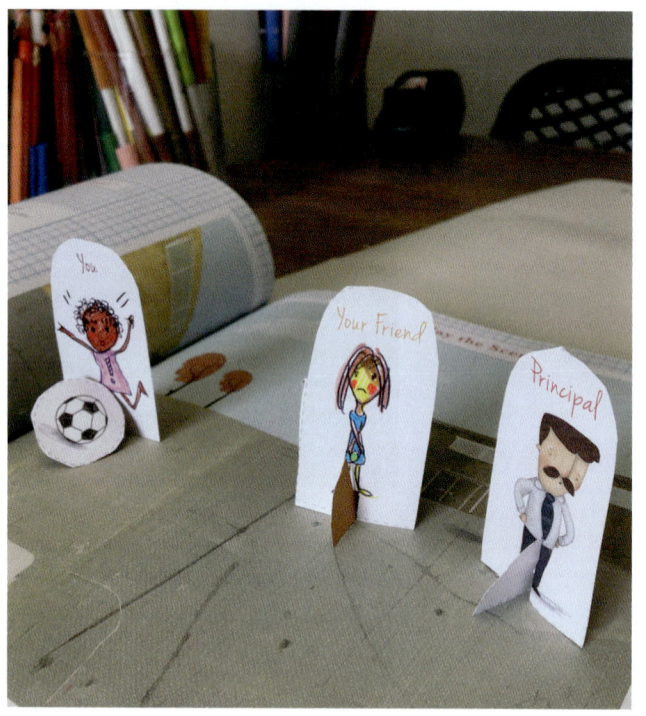

Resource courtesy of the Best of Friends program (O'Brien, 2017)

Step 1: Ask students to create a scene that has occurred in their playground where there were different points of view. Use paper, leaves or tree bark to make the characters involved and any props, like a tiny soccer ball or similar, to set the scene.

Step 2: Ask students to consider more than one point of view by looking at the scene from different angles. Explain the event from each character's perspective.

Step 3: Now, create a different ending for the story. Try to make it fair for everyone.

CASE STUDY

Damien (9): Loud leadership

Damien is impulsive and he often talks over others when he has something to share. Working in groups is a challenge for Damien because he would prefer to have things his own way, rather than gaining the consensus of all group members.

Compared to his peers, Damien's voice is loud and he doesn't encourage others to contribute. Instead, Damien thinks the quiet members of his group agree with everything he suggests. He is surprised when his educator stops their group project to remind Damien to advocate for the rights of others and to make fair or equitable decisions.

Damien does not know how to do this. He feels frustrated with his group for not doing and saying more. Telling them what to do seems like the only solution. Isn't that what leaders are supposed to do?

How to help Damien

1. Ask the whole class to revise their group rules at the beginning and middle of any team project. To ensure every student has an opportunity to contribute, ask each student to write down their ideal group rules before sharing them with each other. A long list of group rules is better than excluding good ideas.

2. Suggest non-verbal group activities to reduce Damien's dependence on his voice. This will give other group members a chance to contribute using drawings or other visual props, like graphs or similar, to express an idea in a different way.

3. Introduce background music during group tasks to help Damien's voice blend in to the environment and to potentially reduce his frustration.

4. Give Damien the role of scribe and ask him to record the ideas of others. Praise his efforts at listening.

5. Recommended children's books about teamwork and generosity:
    - *Stone Soup* by Jon J Muth
    - *The Great Big Enormous Turnip* by Alexei Tolstoy and Helen Oxenbury

DR KIMBERLEY'S TOP 5 TIPS

To encourage advocacy and consensus

1 Promote listening and observing as the most essential aspects of understanding.
2 Use examples to explain a range of situations where there is an *imbalance of power*. Examples include:
   - native animals vs logging companies
   - Indigenous tribes vs European settlers
   - street kids vs police.
3 Consider the rights of the less powerful people in the situation and why their needs are equally important.
4 Challenge students to speak on behalf of those whose voices are not being heard.
5 Ask students to propose an idea to help rebalance the power, and put their suggestions on display.

■ Activity 2: How to advocate for yourself and others at school

Step 1: In a speech bubble (see below), ask students to write their best idea to make things fair for everybody at the school. For example, 'If I were in charge of this school, I would …'

Step 2: In thought bubbles, students should write the thoughts of a student or educator in the audience as they are hearing their idea. What would they think?

Advocating for yourself and others

Step 3: If you have access to a sound or video recorder, ask students to create a 30-second speech using their own voice to advocate for themselves and others at the school who they perceive to be less powerful.

Step 4: After you have finished recording, suggest to students that they could send the video or sound recording to the principal if they would like him or her to consider their ideas about how to make the school a better place. This is called *advocating* and most leaders appreciate the suggestions of young people.

Most leaders appreciate suggestions from young people

Social and emotional intelligence

Some children and adults are more interested than others in the social and emotional world around them. Observing social situations is an excellent way to develop social and emotional intelligence. By watching people, we can try to understand why they are feeling a certain way and how others are likely to behave in any given situation.

Connecting with another person goes beyond saying 'please' and 'thank you' – for example, when we purchase something from a shop assistant. To make an impression on another person requires the use of eye contact and a genuine interest in how that person may be feeling. Given the number of children and adults who spend their days in schools, educators are incredibly fortunate to have many opportunities to help children develop their social and emotional intelligence. Making it fun is a great place to start!

CASE STUDY

Stephanie (10): Inconsistent friendships

Stephanie is having trouble with her friends. They have known each other since Kindergarten and now it feels like they all need a change. Stephanie spends most lunchtimes trying to make sure everyone is getting along. When trouble erupts, Stephanie usually tells the teacher because she does not want to choose between her friends.

Most lunchtimes end the same way. Someone is angry at Stephanie for telling the teacher and the teacher tells Stephanie, 'Sort it out yourselves'. The problem is Stephanie can't sort it out. She feels loyal to her friendship group, but they are no longer making her happy. Trying to find another group sounds easy, but Stephanie can't seem to find a way in.

Stephanie's parents think going to a new school might solve things in the short term, but there must be a better way to take control of this situation. For Stephanie, playing has never been so exhausting and this does not seem to be a passing phase.

How to help Stephanie

1 Consider reading and completing the activities in Hodder Education's *PYP ATL Skills Workbook: Social and Emotional Intelligence and Emotional Management* resource for children in primary school (www.hoddereducation.com/ib-pyp).

2 You, as the educator, are encouraged to invite Stephanie and her parents to a meeting to reassure them of your support and commitment to resolve the friendship issues together. Suggest that Stephanie builds a network of friends outside of school to maintain her self-esteem and to provide positive social options after school and on weekends.

3 Research local social opportunities that might interest Stephanie, such as Girl Scouts, circus skills or a robotics class. Send links to share information with Stephanie's parents.

4 Introduce Stephanie to older and younger students by giving her roles and responsibilities during breaks, such as showing a new student around or helping to set up for assembly, to give her time away from her usual social group.

5 Praise Stephanie for taking care of herself during breaks by not 'trying to keep everyone happy'. She will learn to walk away when tensions build between her peers.

6 Consider reading Hodder's *PYP Friends* storybooks (www.hoddereducation.com/ib-pyp), focusing on interpersonal relationships, social engagement, managing conflict and making new friends. The storybooks also have activities to boost social skills.

Chapter 4 ATL skills: Social skills

Disagreements within friendship groups can be a source of unhappiness

DR KIMBERLEY'S TOP 5 TIPS

To boost social and emotional intelligence

1. Map your emotions over the course of a day to better understand your triggers.
2. After every emotional reaction, practise expressing what happened in words.

3 Develop techniques to regulate your emotions. Examples include:
- Open a window and take a breath of fresh air.
- Walk to the bathroom and be alone.
- Go outside and move around.

4 Observe others from a distance to develop social awareness. Looking down on a crowd from above or through a window will give you space to study body language and group dynamics without engaging.

5 Practise social skills by walking past groups. Use non-verbal greetings to connect, such as a smile, wave or nod. Take time to observe in a social situation before participating. This also allows time to listen to the voice tones and volume of others. This is similar to listening to the start of a song to get a feel for the rhythm.

Most educators experience a range of emotions throughout the day. You may even wish to consider the feelings you experienced earlier in the day to share with your class as an example of emotional intelligence. It is an opportunity to show that all humans have 'ups and downs' and, over time, everything changes eventually, even feelings we thought may never change.

Here is an example of how to map your emotions using visual resources:

Mapping your emotions using visual resources. The timeline is drawn first, and then the visuals are added. The words are added last to describe each step of the event

Chapter 4 ATL skills: Social skills

Here is another example using natural resources:

Mapping your emotions using natural resources. This concept of using nature-based resources for social and emotional learning (SEL) was developed by Dr Kimberley O'Brien (2019)

■ Activity 3: How to map your feelings

Most people find it easier to remember a recent period of time, especially when mapping different feelings in detail.

Step 1: Ask your students to think about their morning. What happened before school and how did they feel about it?

Step 2: Show the students an example of a feelings timeline and ask them to create their own.

Step 3: Ask students to share the ups and downs with a friend or partner, to practise talking about emotions and the influence of other people on our feelings. Being considerate of others is a key part of social and emotional intelligence.

CHAPTER 5

ATL skills: Communication skills

> **IN A NUTSHELL**
> - Communicating is much bigger than speaking. This chapter highlights the importance of effective listening, interpreting and speaking.
> - This chapter provides case studies illustrating the difficulties children often encounter with limited communication skills.
> - Dr Kimberley's Top 5 Tips give teachers practical tools for avoiding common communication pitfalls and improving their own listening, interpreting and speaking skills in the classroom, as well as serving as effective models to students.
> - Activities to boost listening, interpreting and speaking skills are explained to assist educators in bringing out these new skills in students.

Communication skills go beyond our vocabulary and confidence as a speaker. By tuning into non-verbal cues, body language and the dynamics between people, we are able to articulate the nuances and emotions that make for interesting discussion and greater understanding. This chapter will explore three aspects of communication: listening, interpreting and speaking.

In the school context, regular and respectful communication between parents and educators is essential for students to maintain loyalty and a sense of belonging at home and school. Without consistency between parents and educators, children often feel conflicted, particularly if parents or educators speak negatively about the other.

A solid relationship with the parent community will often foster a faster connection with students. Children who trust your intentions will tell you what they are thinking and feeling. Being present, calm and kind can be done silently. Giving young people the space to think and the time to put their thoughts together will often result in a short burst of powerful words with much emotion, or questions for you to slowly ponder together.

Listening

Listening allows us to focus on the retention of new information and gives us the chance to form skilful questions. Good listening sends a powerful message to those who are speaking. It is the basis of a meaningful connection and allows us to establish deeper personal relationships.

CASE STUDY

Ben (12): Fast worker

Ben is a high achiever. He always does well in exams and has the certificates to prove it. In class, Ben likes to participate, but he finds it difficult to listen to his peers. Ben would like to have a direct line to his educator without any distractions, but there are 22 other students in the room.

Ben feels hurt when he is asked to wait. He also feels stuck, frustrated and unable to move forward. He told his parents and they have arranged a meeting with his teacher. Ben is not sure if this is a good thing.

Now Ben is worried about the meeting and he is not feeling happy in class. He has stopped listening to the class discussion and he rarely participates or bothers to answer questions. Ben wants his teacher to like him, and staying quiet seems to make it easier for her.

How to help Ben

1. Ben's educator may have noticed a decline in his class participation and would do well to share this observation with Ben to gain his feedback. Reassuring Ben that his contributions are very important and helpful from an educator's perspective may help to boost his self-esteem and class participation.

2. Give Ben a role or responsibility, such as collecting, analysing and interpreting data or information gathered during class discussions to feed back to the class. Teaching Ben how to do this may require an investment of time but the results will be long term.

3. Ben is likely to excel in an extension class or similar academic opportunity. If these are not available at your school, research options in the community, such as Gifted and Talented school holiday programs or similar short courses at local universities or online. For additional resources to share with Ben's parents, go to: **http://www.mensaforkids.org/**

4. Ben would do well to have a Challenge Box or Challenge File filled with more advanced academic worksheets for him to access after completing the core curriculum activities. This will give him a plan and motivation to continue working at his own pace.

5. Suggest Ben uses a Question Book to record any questions he may have while his educator is working with other students. This will ensure the questions are valued and can be answered in one discussion when the educator is available.

6. A recommended children's book for high achievers:
   - *Terrific Ways to Stretch Your Brain* by Evelyn B Christensen

DR KIMBERLEY'S TOP 5 TIPS

To boost listening skills

1 Find value in every student's contribution and articulate extra depth or real-life examples to their responses where possible. This will keep the class engaged.

2 Use sound bites or parts of podcasts to immerse students in diverse audio context.

3 Ensure there are regular periods of silence to give children a break from stimulation. Aim for a minimum of three minutes every half hour.

4 Encourage quiet students to write their suggestions on paper for you to articulate on their behalf, or use an online survey, email responses or similar.

5 If students are talking over or interrupting others, point it out *every single time*. If a student talks over you, cease what you are saying immediately and freeze. Raising your voice will not solve this issue, only silence and non-verbal cues will draw attention to this behavioural issue. Praise patience.

■ Activity 1: How to host a Listening Tour

Step 1: Divide students into groups of 4–5 and ask each group to think of a question that impacts everybody at school, including all the staff, parents and students. Some examples include,

- How could we make our school more peaceful?
- How could we make every school bathroom even better?
- How could our school community be even more supportive?

Step 2: Ask students to go on a Listening Tour by asking as many students, parents and staff from all parts of the school their question. Students should record all suggestions in writing or as part of an audio recording.

Step 3: In their original groups, students should share all the diverse responses and find themes by placing similar suggestions in the same pile. Each group should create a visual display to share the outcome of their Listening Tour with the rest of the class.

Here is an example of an infographic for the results of a Listening Tour:

Chapter 5 ATL skills: Communication skills

How to make our school more peaceful

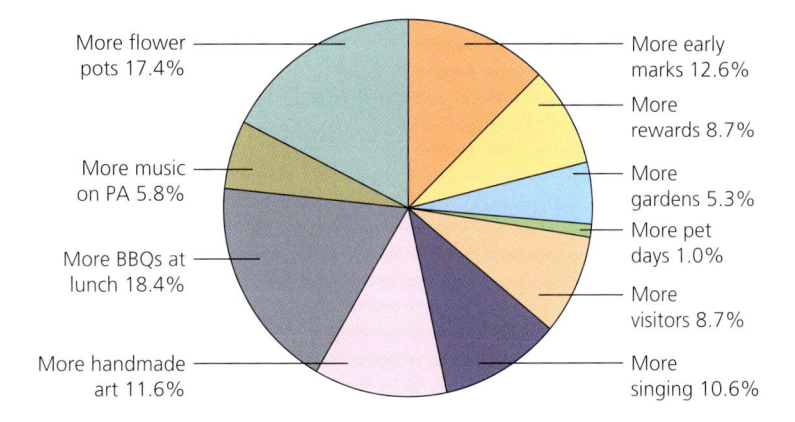

- More flower pots 17.4%
- More music on PA 5.8%
- More BBQs at lunch 18.4%
- More handmade art 11.6%
- More early marks 12.6%
- More rewards 8.7%
- More gardens 5.3%
- More pet days 1.0%
- More visitors 8.7%
- More singing 10.6%

This is another example of an infographic that students could use to present findings from their Listening Tour:

Result from a student's Listening Tour

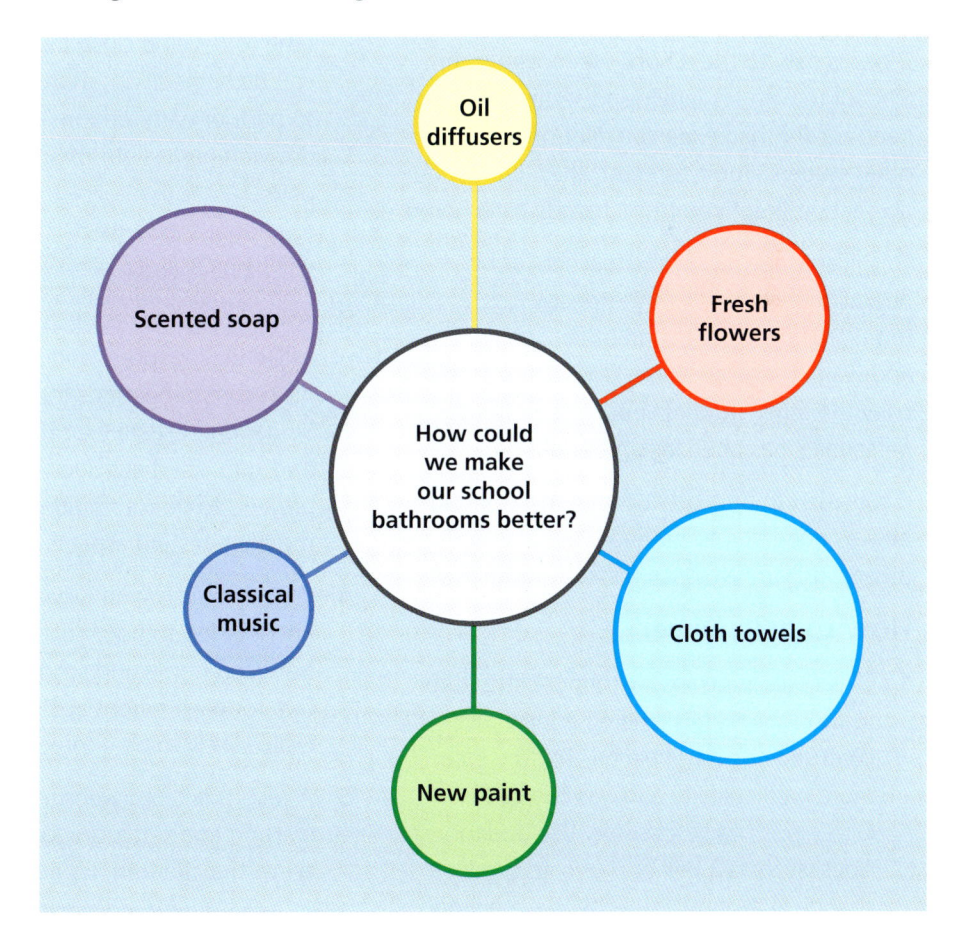

How could we make our school bathrooms better?
- Oil diffusers
- Fresh flowers
- Cloth towels
- New paint
- Classical music
- Scented soap

Interpreting

Most students require local knowledge to derive meaning from what they see and hear in their learning environment. Being familiar with a school includes knowing the educators and other students well enough to recognize their voices, and to have a fairly good understanding of their personalities. Local knowledge also extends to being able to identify bird sounds and background noises, such as aeroplanes, freight trains and buses idling at the bus stop. All these sights and sounds inform our senses. Being able to interpret visual, audio and oral communication is essential as we become comfortable and able to retain new information.

CASE STUDY

Oliver (8): Lost in translation

Oliver is new to the school. He moved from Singapore with his family and settling in has been harder than expected. Not only do the other students look different, they also sound and act differently from his friends back home.

To Oliver, it seems like the teachers at his new school have different expectations too. Some make jokes and others watch and wait for silence. Oliver does his best to copy the other students but he feels like his personality has been lost in translation.

Oliver used to be a great communicator and he was good at interpreting what was going on around him. Now, Oliver is overwhelmed.

How to help Oliver

1. Oliver would do well with more structure to fill in the blanks where he feels confused or overwhelmed. Try to create more predictability and less choice for Oliver in his daily schedule. Use auditory clues, such as a bell or music, to signify a change in routine, rather than expecting students to know what comes next.

2. Oliver, like most new students, will take time to develop close friendships. This can be helped with more opportunities to partner with random classmates. Try drawing names out of a basket to allocate pairs, rather than allowing the students to choose the same partner as usual. This will help Oliver to meet new people.

3. Ask the class to research 'Five Fun Things to Do in Singapore' and ask Oliver to share his recommendations for children visiting Singapore. Create brochures with pictures and suggested activities for families, or pretend to be tour guides and explain the most interesting aspects of Singapore.

4. Weekly emails with Oliver's parents are encouraged to boost communication between home and school. A new role for each parent in Oliver's school is also likely to be appreciated.

5. A recommended website for choosing, starting and settling into a new school:
    - raisingchildren.net.au/school-age/school-learning/school-choosing-starting-moving/starting-school

DR KIMBERLEY'S TOP 5 TIPS

To interpret visual, audio and oral communication

1. Break communication down into three different streams of information:
   - visual (eg: body language, non-verbal cues and hand gestures)
   - audio (eg: school bells, footsteps, furniture moving and garden sprinklers)
   - oral (eg: voice tone, volume, pitch, sighing, throat clearing and the spoken content)
2. Take time to listen and decipher the different noises with your students. A tour upstairs, downstairs and around the building to explain the sources of every sound is always a settling experience for newcomers.
3. Ask about differences in cultures. Jokes from a teacher may not be culturally appropriate in some settings. Explore other differences, such as hand gestures, with curiosity and let the students lead the discussion.
4. Think about the influence of movement and body language on communication. Some teachers move rapidly, others are virtually still. Ask the students for their opinion on your body language. You may be surprised how it makes them feel. Feedback is power!
5. Experiment with using only one type of communication at a time. For example, make all your lessons visual by using demonstrations rather than verbal explanations. Ask your students to vote on their favourite way to interpret information – visual, audio or oral.

Do	Don't
✔ Stand up straight	✘ Fold your arms
✔ Use the whole classroom	✘ Stand behind a desk or barrier
✔ Indicate approval with a nod	✘ Look at your watch when a child is speaking
✔ Smile to convey happiness and encouragement	✘ Frown
✔ Make eye contact	✘ Rush students
✔ Raise your hand to speak	✘ Stand over students
✔ Put your hand on your chin when asking students to think	✘ Sit on the desk of a student
✔ Use open palms and wait for more than 10 seconds before taking the first response to a question	✘ Ignore a waiting student
	✘ Intimidate
	✘ Encroach on personal space
	✘ Insist on eye contact
	✘ Put your back to students

Body language for educators

■ Activity 2: How to record a soundscape

Step 1: The educator and students will require a sound recorder, such as a voice memo app on a mobile phone or a small audio recording device.

Step 2: Walk around the school collecting a range of different noises. Students could also do this at weekends or after school for a more diverse collection of sounds.

Step 3: Return to the classroom, amplify the recording devices (eg, use a Bluetooth speaker or similar) and take turns sharing the sounds. Ask students to guess what each sound is and where it was recorded.

A student collecting sounds using an audio recorder

CASE STUDY

Taj (5): Tongue tied

Taj is very articulate and he tends to speak more when he is anxious or excited. Taj often interrupts his mother when she starts a conversation with someone new, and then he has trouble expressing himself clearly and logically.

The same thing happens when Taj is in class. He cannot seem to untangle all of his ideas when he is under pressure, such as when he is called on to answer a question or share news in front of the class.

Taj's parents and educators know he is intelligent but his ability to state his opinions, speak about his ideas and negotiate effectively do not reflect his true potential. To top it all off, Taj's self-esteem is being impacted and he has no idea how to fix it.

How to help Taj

1 Encourage more one-to-one conversations with Taj to build a trusting teacher–student relationship.

2 Help Taj to create a mind map to help him visualize the contents of the speech or news item he plans to share with the class. Encourage Taj to use the map as a prop while he is talking so he keeps on track with his plan.

3 Praise his efforts to continue trying.

4 Ask Taj to record his ideas on an audio file to see if he is more articulate without an audience. Help Taj to transcribe the audio recording into notes and suggest he refers to this script during his speech for added confidence.

5 Practise relaxation strategies as a class to help manage Taj's anxiety. See Chapter 7 in this book for ideas, or refer to Hodder Education's *PYP ATL Skills Workbook: Mindfulness* resource for children, available at www.hoddereducation.com/ib-pyp

DR KIMBERLEY'S TOP 5 TIPS

To speak and express ideas clearly

1 Decide on one idea you would like to express.
2 Brainstorm all of your thoughts regarding this idea. Record each thought in a bubble around the central idea. This is called a mind map.
3 Sequence each thought along a timeline to make some sense of them.
4 Cross out any thoughts which do not add to the story or central idea.
5 Practise and memorize each point on the timeline. Use a picture or word to symbolize each thought. Now you are ready to add hand gestures, pauses and some emphasis. Have fun!

Wellbeing for the IB PYP: Teaching for Success

■ Activity 3: A train of thought

Step 1: Use a stimulus picture to spark some thoughts without giving any verbal explanation of the image.

Example of a stimulus picture

Step 2: Ask students to brainstorm and record all their ideas that are triggered by the image.

Step 3: Put the ideas in a sequence to create a story or speech. Delete or edit any thoughts that detract or move in a different direction from the other ideas. Practise expressing the thoughts clearly and logically. Present when ready!

CHAPTER 6

ATL skills: Self-management skills

IN A NUTSHELL

- Self-management skills include emotional regulation, perseverance and resilience. Children come to school with different skills in self-management and may sometimes lack insight into the triggers for their emotions.
- Case studies and activities within this chapter assist children to:
  - ☐ identify the triggers to emotions
  - ☐ think creatively about how to persevere through difficulty
  - ☐ build self-efficacy around their own capacity to be resilient.
- Educators may also find the lack of control over curriculum and workplace conditions challenging to resilience. This chapter highlights how fostering a culture of wellbeing within the classroom can buffer against challenges outside the classroom.
- Dr Kimberley's Top 5 Tips identify specific behaviours for educators to model in class and to help with remedying challenging behaviours.

What are self-management skills?

Self-management skills include emotional regulation, perseverance and resilience. Being able to manage your emotions, demonstrate persistence, remove barriers, engage in positive thinking and motivate yourself to find a solution, or cope with the consequences, is all part of good self-management.

Resilience is another key aspect of self-management. Being able to manage setbacks, work through adversity, process disappointments and accept change are all essential aspects of self-management. This chapter provides activities for educators based on case studies illustrating common issues related to the challenges students often experience as they develop their capacity to regulate emotions, persevere and practise resilience.

Self-management includes developing skills to regulate our emotions

Emotional regulation

CASE STUDY

Summer (10): Meltdowns in the morning

Summer is sensitive to the seams in her socks. She is not fond of having her hair brushed, and being rushed out the door to school can trigger a meltdown. Summer's meltdowns are monumental. She cries loudly, hides behind furniture or under her desk and occasionally runs away.

Summer's parents are used to this behaviour, but her educators often lack the time and resources required to manage Summer. In Kindergarten, her meltdowns included biting and kicking, but now Summer is more likely to hide for up to 45 minutes until she is ready to reappear.

Occasionally, Summer shows insight and can articulate what triggered her behaviour and why. She is more able to manage her feelings and cope with consequences at school, but Summer lacks the maturity of her same-aged peers. More help is required for Summer to develop coping skills at home and school.

How to help Summer

1. Summer would do well to have a calm space to help her integrate the triggers in her environment, such as background noise, with her emotional needs. Summer should be encouraged to use this space rather than hide behind furniture or run away. Noise-cancelling headphones and sensory toys, such as Nail Art, may help Summer to settle.

2. Further testing by a psychologist and an occupational therapist is recommended, to better understand Summer's sensory avoidant behaviour and to support her parents and educators to better manage meltdowns.

3. Praise Summer when she returns from her calm space in less than 45 minutes, working towards a personal best (PB) for coping. Graph Summer's time in the calm space over the course of a month to review her progress, using rewards to optimize engagement and motivation.

4. Occupational therapists often recommend weighted lap blankets to help settle students with sensory issues. For further details, send Summer's parents a link to explore sensory tools, such as: **https://sensorytools.net**

5. Weekly emails with Summer's parents and monthly meetings at the school are encouraged to share her progress and to ensure educators, parents and allied health professionals can regularly review their shared goals for Summer.

6. A recommended book for parents and educators to help prevent meltdowns is:
   - *No More Meltdowns* by Jed Baker.

NB: Nail Art is a resource often used to engage children with traits of Autism Spectrum Disorder.

For more information, go to **www.nationalautismresources.com/pin-art/**

DR KIMBERLEY'S TOP 5 TIPS
To practise emotional regulation
1. Use words to calmly describe any rising tension or uncomfortable feelings of overwhelm. This is modelling good emotional regulation.
2. Encourage students to know what they need to calm down and offer a variety of options, such as a calm zone under a tree, or in a private and comfy swing or hammock.
3. Show insight after regulating your emotions, such as, 'I was getting bothered before, but after I stood in front of the fan, I felt cooler and calmer.'
4. Praise a child who returns from the calm zone for regulating their emotions.
5. Think of structured roles or responsibilities to give to children who need help to settle, like feeding the fish, watering the plants or picking flowers. Scheduling these jobs early in the day as part of the daily ritual will give emotional children more tolerance.

■ Activity 1: Emotional regulation cartoon

Step 1: Teach children to know their emotional triggers. Brainstorm 'What sets you off emotionally?' and give some of your own examples, including what triggers your anxiety (eg, losing your keys), what triggers excitement (eg, a surprise party) and what triggers your anger (eg, a mess in the kitchen).

Step 2: Of the ideas brainstormed in step 1, ask students to choose one emotion they would most like to regulate or manage more carefully.

Now, ask students to draw the *exact instance* their chosen emotion is triggered before they react.

Step 3: Ask students to draw two different cartoons using a 'before, during and after' sequence. Insert two different reactions to the same problem to achieve two different outcomes.

On the next page, there are two examples of emotional regulation cartoons.

1 Without planning, being called on at assembly can trigger tears

Before — Teacher calls my name at assembly.
During — I cry.
After — I look like a mess.

2 With planning, the same trigger is manageable and emotions are regulated

Before — I ask if I will get my name called out.
During — I am ready!
After — I am proud!

Perseverance

Perseverance is not giving up, even when things are difficult. Being persistent and tenacious enough to maintain the effort required to complete a task is perseverance. Some children find it easier than others to push through challenges in order to reach their goals. Those who struggle to persevere are often accustomed to accessing help and they feel fearful of failure when trying something new.

Children learn to persevere with practice and small successes. Parents and educators can encourage, model and highlight instances of perseverance, but there are limits to these approaches. Children need to be self-motivated to persevere, and for some children, particularly those who may be sensitive and highly intelligent, getting things wrong may be traumatic and something to be avoided.

CASE STUDY

Lollima (8): The perfectionist

Lollima gives up easily and is resistant to learning new skills. She does not like to fail, whether she is learning to ride a bike or copying a picture from a book. The thought of making a mistake triggers Lollima's anxiety. She would rather refuse to try than to get it wrong.

Lollima's teacher has tried reassuring her and she always praises effort over outcome, but Lollima rarely allows herself to start a new task, making it difficult to reward her attempts. Instead, Lollima withdraws and shakes her head. With too much attention or prompting, Lollima starts to cry.

At home, Lollima's parents are equally frustrated and sympathetic. They are also concerned about her lack of progress academically. Psychometric testing revealed Lollima has a high average IQ, but without engagement, persistence and greater resilience she is unlikely to reach her learning potential.

How to help Lollima

1 Lollima is likely to do better when given more time to complete tasks. She may also feel reassured if shown an example of the work she is required to do. Give her a week to work on a very small task and avoid encouraging her during this period. Lollima may surprise you.

2 Further testing by a psychologist with an individual achievement test will determine Lollima's strengths and weaknesses in terms of writing, reading, listening comprehension and oral expression. If Lollima completes even part of the test, it will be possible to find her preferred learning style. She may avoid writing, but love listening or using her voice to express herself.

3 Design classroom activities to harness Lollima's strengths. This will build her confidence with starting new tasks and give you something to praise.

4 Introduce some new board games or card games to your class. This may boost Lollima's participation and her status among her peers.

5 Weekly emails with Lollima's parents and monthly meetings at the school are encouraged in order to share Lollima's progress. She may be eligible for learning support if there are minimal improvements to report. Small group learning and tutoring is often better for children who are overcoming perfectionism and working on coping skills.

6 A recommended children's book about perfectionism:
   - *Nobody's Perfect* by Ellen Flanagan

Some children find it easier than others to take on new challenges

DR KIMBERLEY'S TOP 5 TIPS

To develop perseverance

1 Build from small successes in quick succession to a slightly greater challenge. This will build trust, increase risk-taking and will help to sustain perseverance.

2 Read children's books about perseverance and grit to normalize the challenges associated with trying for a long period of time to achieve a goal.

3 Watch multiple tutorials on YouTube to learn different versions of the same skill. Use slow motion if necessary and see which one your students prefer. Three tutorials to make a paper plane include: 'How to make an Easy Paper Plane that Flies Far' www.youtube.com/watch?v=AljTDb2cyhc, 'The plane that flies long' www.youtube.com/watch?v=-PlkNStPDQU, 'How to make the BEST paper airplane jet' www.youtube.com/watch?v=bHglySrR5vs.

4 Schedule time to practise for periods of 30 seconds to 30 minutes. Start where the child is comfortable and increase incrementally over time. Use a timer to signify when practice is complete, regardless of the child's achievements.

5 Use phrases such as 'making progress' to model positive self-talk and self-motivation.

Chapter 6 ATL skills: Self-management skills

■ Activity 2: Perseverance lucky dip

In some areas of life, it is easier to persevere, like finishing a race even though you are tired at your school's sports carnival. In other areas, it can be difficult, like cleaning up your room before your friend can come to visit.

Step 1: Write 10 different scenarios which may require perseverance on small, separate pieces of paper. Fold them and place each scenario in a hat or bowl.

Step 2: One by one, ask a student to pull a scenario out of the hat and ask: 'How easy would it be for you to persevere in this situation?' and, 'How would you find a way to persevere?'

Step 3: After each response, ask the class: 'What would make it easier for you to persevere?' Take note of their ideas and put these on display for future reference.

Examples of scenarios which require perseverance

- Learning to swim
- Learning an instrument
- Making your own breakfast
- Cleaning your room
- Riding a bike
- Trying to get your pen licence
- Reading 'Harry Potter'
- Getting dressed without help
- Learning to make spaghetti
- Styling your own hair
- Sweeping the floor
- Tying your shoelaces
- Meeting new people

Resilience

Resilience is the ability to adapt and grow from a difficult challenge or adversity. It is a skill that can be developed with practice, and it is one that most educators require in abundance. In fact, *teacher resilience* has attracted much research in recent years, with two out of three new teachers changing professions within their first five years of teaching (Boe *et al.*, 2008; Keigher, Cross, 2010; Landy, Conte, 2013; Lindqvist *et al.*, 2014).

Interestingly, these statistics are similar in Australia, the US and the UK, with factors such as having little influence over the curriculum and workplace conditions cited as reasons for leaving the profession. Educators with the most resilience cited more control and support in the school setting as the top two reasons for greater job satisfaction. Children also thrive from a sense of control and support. It gives them a reason to stay and to keep on trying. Fostering wellbeing in classrooms is where educators have the most control and the greatest capacity to emotionally support themselves and their students.

CASE STUDY

Zac (6): Limited resilience

Zac is easily triggered by the decisions of his educator. If he is not chosen for a special task, like being the leader, he feels slighted and may yell, 'That's not fair!' He looks upset and angry but his peers are used to his reactions. He has a reputation for being emotionally reactive.

Zac usually needs some time in the bathroom to recover. He splashes his face and returns red-eyed to the classroom after 10–20 minutes, with his head lowered, walking quickly to his chair. At home, Zac receives more support when he cries. His mother tries to help Zac hide his tears when friends are visiting. She apologizes on his behalf.

Most of the other children in Zac's class can cope with setbacks or disappointment. Zac does not like getting upset, but it is a habit he is finding hard to break. It seems like every time he misses out or doesn't win, all the same old feelings keep flooding back.

How to help Zac

1 Praise Zac when he recovers from a setback. Encourage him to express his disappointment using calm words, rather than yelling, if he is open to feedback after an incident.

2 Give Zac and his classmates more roles and responsibilities to reduce competition related to being selected. Ideally, find a role for every class member and rotate these regularly. Most children love using a broom or a wheelbarrow. Make it more fun by inventing a 'Broom Licence' or a 'Wheelbarrow Licence' to increase the status of each new responsibility.

3 Meet with Zac's parents and normalize resilience as a skill we all need to learn. Share Zac's progress and encourage a sharing approach by only focusing on how long it takes him to bounce back or recover from a setback.

4 Encourage weekly email communication to monitor his improvements together, at home and at school.

5 Encourage Zac's parents not to avoid exposing Zac to potential setbacks or triggers, and to be open about his improvements, rather than being secretive or apologetic about his coping skills.

6 Zac's educators would do well to introduce resources to increase emotional literacy in the classroom. *Face It* cards are used to encourage students and educators to use a broader range of words to explain different facial expressions. This will help to develop Zac's emotional vocabulary and his ability to use words to express his emotions. For details, see: **therapeuticresources.com.au/products/face-it**

DR KIMBERLEY'S TOP 5 TIPS
To boost resilience

1 Encourage children to put their challenges into perspective. Like a chapter in a book, a person's life story has many highs and lows, including interesting obstacles to overcome on a journey of self-discovery. Enjoy the ride!

2 Navigate every new challenge like a detective with a new crime to solve. Start looking for clues that might help you work out the way forward. Other people may have experienced something similar – ask friends, family members, neighbours and educators how they would tackle the situation. Put the pieces together to reveal a solution.

3 Take baby steps towards your goal. Making progress will build your confidence and, before long, you will be on the other side.

4 Reward yourself for effort – new challenges are always confronting. Being kind to yourself will give you the stamina to continue.

5 Picture the results you would like to achieve! Visualize it in detail. Imagine what you will see, hear, smell and taste when you reach your goal. Do this every day and consider every tiny step along the way so it feels more real. With good preparation, you will know exactly what to expect when your moment comes.

■ Activity 3: Capture the moment

Use children's stories of resilience to spark ideas for this activity. Here are two examples:

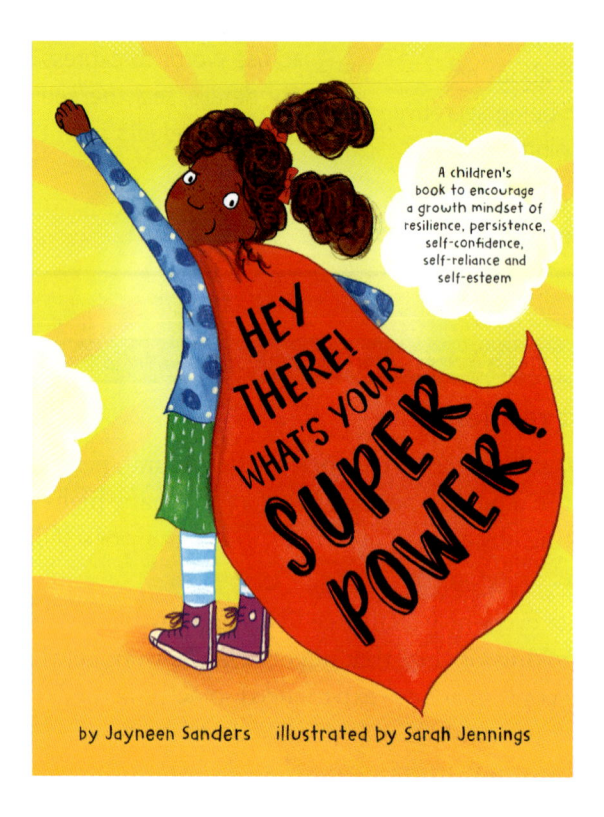

- Van Cuylenburg, H. 2019. *The Resilience Project: Finding Happiness Through Gratitude & Mindfulness.* Melbourne. Penguin Random House
- Sanders, J and Jennings, S. 2019. *Hey There! What's Your Superpower?* Victoria. Educate2Empower Publishing (pictured)

Step 1: Ask the students to think of 'a moment you surprised yourself'. Some examples may include saving a sibling, helping a stranger, or caring about something more than usual.

Step 2: Draw a picture to capture that moment of resilience.

Step 3: Ask your students to think about a personal strength or *superpower* that has helped them to be more resilient. Write their superpower on their picture and display in the foyer of the school or in the library for all to see!

CHAPTER 7

Anxiety, stress and mindfulness

> **IN A NUTSHELL**
> - Most educators around the world experience stress and anxiety in the workplace, with Japanese elementary school teachers working the longest hours.
> - Children are also becoming increasingly anxious due to overscheduling, excessive screen time, parental conflict, financial stress and high expectations.
> - In this chapter, the signs of stress and anxiety in children are listed and a case study is used to illustrate common symptoms of stress in students.
> - Mindfulness is gaining traction as a self-management skill to extend concentration and reduce distractibility among students.
> - Dr Kimberley shares her Top 5 Tips for educators to manage stress and anxiety among students and how to implement mindfulness in schools.
> - This chapter also shows educators how to create a weekly visualization in a step-by-step activity to use in classrooms.
> - Children who practise mindfulness meditation on a regular basis are more able to let thoughts and feelings pass without reacting or judging each sensation as positive or negative.
> - Research suggests that students who practise mindfulness are more self-aware and are better able to regulate their emotions.
> - Resources, such as free children's meditations, are shared, including Insight Timer and Smiling Minds.

Anxiety and stress are part of daily life for many adults juggling the responsibilities of working, studying and fulfilling commitments in the modern world, alongside raising children for some. Knowing how to counteract the onset of stress is necessary to achieve a restful eight hours of sleep, good digestion and enough relaxation to achieve physical health and psychological wellbeing.

According to the results of the 2019 Teacher Wellbeing Index (UK), 72% of educators described themselves as stressed, and 74% of education professionals considered their inability to switch off and relax to be the major contributing factor to a negative work/life balance. Of those surveyed, 34% of teachers worked more than 51 hours per week. In Mongolia, teachers work a maximum of 40 hours per week (UNICEF Mongolia, 2012).

Wellbeing for the IB PYP: Teaching for Success

Many educators struggle to find a positive work/life balance

Japanese elementary or primary school teachers work the longest hours of any country, with an average of 54.4 hours per week, according to the 2018 results of the Teaching and Learning International Survey (TALIS) conducted by the Organisation for Economic Co-operation and Development (OECD). This research involved 260 000 teachers in 15 000 schools across 48 countries (OECD, 2019).

Anxiety and stress in childhood

Since we opened in 2007, anxiety is the single most common reason parents refer their children to our services at Quirky Kid psychology clinics. More and more children are experiencing physical or behavioural changes, such as toileting issues and avoidance, often triggered by anxiety. Parents and educators may overlook the underlying factors that lead to these changes, including overscheduling, excessive screen time, parental conflict, financial stress and high expectations.

SIGNS OF STRESS AND ANXIETY IN CHILDREN

Behavioural changes

- Difficulty concentrating
- Aggression
- Clinginess
- Fearfulness (fear of the dark, of being alone or of strangers)
- Nail-biting
- Withdrawal from family or friends
- Refusal to go to school
- Pushing boundaries
- Hoarding items of insignificance

Emotional changes

- Moodiness
- Cries easily
- Volatile
- Blaming others
- Sense of hopelessness
- Hypervigilant
- Avoidant

Physical changes

- Decreased or increased appetite
- Complaints of stomach pain or headaches
- Bedwetting
- Sleep problems or nightmares
- Acne, rashes or skin irritations

■ Avoidance of triggers

Children who are anxious or stressed may avoid events, tasks and situations which trigger their worries. Others display more discreet forms of avoidance, such as uncertainty, reassurance-seeking or acting out when confronted by their fears. Most children and adults actively avoid sources of stress or anxiety (Rapee, 2012).

Prevalence rates for anxiety disorders are slightly higher for females than males within Western populations. Although the majority of children will experience some anxiety in childhood, triggered by starting school or being alone in the dark, only 5% of children and adolescents will suffer from a diagnosed anxiety disorder (Rapee, 2012).

CASE STUDY

Michael (11): Anxious and avoidant

Michael had always wanted to do well at school to please his parents. They worked hard to pay his school fees and were depending on Michael's success in later life to make it all worthwhile. When Michael's grades started to slip, he stayed up later to study on a regular basis and often felt tired the next day at school.

He developed eczema, a type of skin irritation inside his elbows and on his fingers. It was incredibly itchy but he tried not to touch the affected skin to prevent bleeding. Michael's friends asked about his eczema and were afraid to touch him in case it was contagious. He started to avoid eating lunch in favour of reading.

Michael had become increasingly lethargic and he was reluctant to play sport at school. His educator was worried that Michael was tired and overscheduled after school. She emailed his parents, but Michael did not think it helped the situation. They told him to go to bed earlier, but with less time to study, his grades were not likely to improve.

In bed, Michael's worries intensified. He could not stop thinking about the opportunities he had been given and how much he did not want the responsibility of supporting his family. Michael felt he did not have anyone to talk to about these thoughts. His parents and educators did not seem to understand.

How to help Michael

1. Michael's educators would do well to invite Michael's parents to be part of a meeting to discuss Michael's anxiety and to determine if the family are experiencing financial stress. If so, encourage Michael's parents not to involve children in discussions regarding finances and ask your school leader to consider offering the family support with school fees, if applicable.

2. Ask Michael and his parents if they would like your help to find a local expert on eczema. If so, research the best GP, pediatrician, skin specialist and child psychologist in the area and share links via email for the family to explore.

3. Suggest a short-term tutor or learning support educator to assist Michal with his study load, organization and scheduling habits in order to avoid late nights.

4. Introduce Michael to the Smiling Mind app (www.smilingmind.com.au) and the relaxation resources in Hodder Education's *Mindfulness: PYP ATL Skills Workbook*, or a similar resource, to encourage visualizations and progressive muscle relaxations (PMR) at bedtime.

5. Offer Michael more structured social opportunities during breaks at school, such as chess club or another club with a topic of interest to him. This will encourage new or closer friendships with like-minded peers.

6. Invite a regular guest yoga teacher to offer students a morning class and encourage Michael to participate to increase his physical activity.

7. Weekly emails between parents and educators are encouraged to monitor Michael's anxiety, eczema, happiness and grades.
8. Fortnightly appointments with a child psychologist or school counsellor may also be a good outlet for Michael to share his thoughts and feelings confidentially. A monthly teleconference between all parties supporting Michael is encouraged for greater consistency.

DR KIMBERLEY'S TOP 5 TIPS
To manage anxiety and stress

1. Take time every day to check in on stress levels with your students as a group. Share your own symptoms of stress or anxiety, such as checking the time or packing up in a fluster. Children will learn to recognize symptoms of stress and how to talk openly about anxiety.
2. Encourage your students to adopt healthy ways to manage stressful situations, including earlier bedtimes, screen limits and seeking out support. Discuss these ideas with your students and brainstorm any barriers together.
3. A picture tells a thousand words. Ask students to find an image of themselves when they were 'most relaxed', and educators are encouraged to do the same. Next, make a list of the ingredients required to create the most relaxed version of yourself. Make them a priority, not optional extras.
4. Reward yourself and your students for effort – listening to an audiobook after lunch may help to bring the stress levels down. Try rating your stress levels pre- and post-relaxation activity. This will give you and your students insight into the benefits for your body and mind.
5. A weekly email from educators to parents is encouraged in order to foster good communication between home and school. This is an excellent opportunity to share what makes your students feel stressed – for example, 'running late', 'forgetting homework' – and what relaxation activities or apps the students most enjoy, in case parents also want to use them at home.

Wellbeing for the IB PYP: Teaching for Success

■ Activity: How to create a weekly visualization

A weekly visualization

Step 1: Create your own visualization that will appeal to your students with the theme of flying away. Magic carpets, hoverboards, wing-suits and jet-packs work well.

This links to an activity in Hodder Education's *PYP ATL Skills Workbook: Mindfulness* – 'Magic Carpet' on page 24.

Step 2: Start your visualization by encouraging students to allow their bodies to fully relax in their seats or on the floor in your classroom. Jump into the story, adding some opportunities for deep breaths, such as, 'Before you zip up your jet pack, take one last giant breath – this is going to be one heck of a ride.'

Step 3: In your visualization, direct your students up and out of the school and head towards the closest ocean, river or mountain range, where the air is fresh. Try to include details to help students engage their senses and their own imaginations.

Step 4: Once you reach approximately one minute into the visualization, give students a few minutes of silence to make their own imaginary side trips before returning to the classroom at the end of the visualization. A maximum of five minutes in total for the visualization is suitable for primary school-aged children.

Mindfulness

Mindfulness is about tuning into the present moment and your own experiences as they happen. In the educational setting, mindfulness is gaining traction as a self-management skill used to extend concentration and reduce distractibility of students. Learning to meditate is producing benefits for children and adults alike.

Without dwelling on the past or worrying about the future, mindfulness encourages children to sharpen their awareness of their body and mind through activities, such as meditation designed for students. By paying attention to certain stimuli and disregarding others, children begin to recognize their own rate of breathing while ignoring background noise, for example.

The positive effects of children's mindfulness meditation on attentional processes is relatively well-documented (Berto, Barbiero, 2014; Felver *et al.*, 2017; Flook *et al.*, 2010). However, the age of the child influences their capacity to engage in a mindfulness activity. Practising yoga or meditation from a young age increases an individual's ability to focus for extended periods (Sheinman *et al.*, 2018).

■ Mindfulness meditation for children

There are many resources for educators interested in learning more about mindfulness meditation for students. Insight Timer has the largest free library of guided meditations (**insighttimer.com/**) and I have heard positive feedback from students, including an increase in their ability to fall asleep using this resource.

A mindfulness meditation encourages children to notice different sensations in their body and new thoughts crossing their mind, without judgment. As mindfulness skills increase, students are more comfortable allowing thoughts and feelings to pass without reacting emotionally.

According to research, primary school-aged children benefit from 30–45 minutes of mindfulness meditation per week. Greater focus and self-awareness among students generally becomes evident after six weeks of practice. Educators who practise mindfulness themselves for approximately 18 minutes per day are more effective at teaching mindfulness (**www.smilingmind.com.au**).

CASE STUDY

Vivien (educator for five years)

Vivien attended a conference and enjoyed a mindfulness meditation as part of a stress management workshop for educators. She would love to incorporate yoga and meditation into her own classroom, given the benefits she experienced first-hand, as a technique to reduce reactivity among her students.

Vivien knows mindfulness is a legitimate part of the school curriculum, but she does not feel qualified enough to facilitate a session without further practice. She also worries what her colleagues may think of mindfulness, and if her students will be open to trying it.

After discussing her idea with the school leaders, Vivien asks a visiting sports coach to offer her class an introduction to yoga and meditation. She agrees, and Vivien participates in the class along with her students. The children are very engaged and their feedback is positive after the lesson.

With the support of her students, Vivien schedules a mindfulness session of yoga and meditation after lunch three days per week. The sessions are initially based on videos she has found online (such as www.cosmickids.com/) but Vivien soon starts to avoid this visual distraction by leading the sessions herself based on the same moves, a period of silence and a time frame of less than 10 minutes.

Vivien's students look forward to the sessions, and she has found significant benefits in terms of their focus and general happiness. They are also less reactive and more patient with each other. Vivien is eager to share her experience with her colleagues, but some are quite negative about mindfulness. She decides to keep the concept to herself.

■ Different perceptions of mindfulness

Attitudes towards meditation are varied. According to Ronald Purser, author of *McMindfulness: How Mindfulness Became the New Capitalist Spirituality*, the idea of waiting for a feeling to pass and focusing on creating your own inner peace neglects the root cause of the issues in society that are impacting on our happiness in the first place.

He cites the example of a business executive working 80 hours per week, who meditates enough to continue working at that rate, while his corporate bosses take no responsibility for the stressful conditions they have created. Purser also encourages activism over acceptance and believes mindfulness undermines the human urge to protest.

Step one is to 'respect resistance' by giving choice. Some students, parents and educators will not wish to participate in mindfulness activities. The right to 'pass' is to be respected, as is the right to participate. Mindfulness as a concept may take some getting used to.

Chapter 7 Anxiety, stress and mindfulness

The origins of mindfulness are connected to Buddhism in countries such as India, where meditation is common practice in many families and communities. Accepting the benefits of yoga and meditation without any reference to religion requires trust in the facilitator and a willingness to test the process. Being open to the feedback and opinions of others is the next step.

Learning to meditate produces benefits for both children and adults

DR KIMBERLEY'S TOP 5 TIPS

To implement mindfulness in schools

1. Gauge the interest of the school community by offering activities such as yoga or meditation at different times of the day to see if parents, educators and students are interested in learning more or participating in regular mindfulness activities.
2. Write an article for the school newsletter (or similar) about mindfulness in classrooms, and invite interested parents or colleagues to contact you. Share evidence-based research and schedule a meet-up.
3. Test out a free mindfulness app yourself and share the results with your school leader. Here's an example: www.smilingmind.com.au/smiling-mind-app
4. Encourage school leaders and colleagues to trial a mindfulness activity at a professional development workshop and request they complete a feedback survey to rate their experience, including any changes in their focus pre- and post-activity.
5. Schedule a daily mindfulness activity for your students. Start with five minutes and see how they respond.

Wellbeing for the IB PYP: Teaching for Success

■ Activity: How to start a mindfulness meditation

Step 1: Ask students to bring their own cushion to their first mindfulness meditation.

Step 2: Pick a time of day that works for you and your students. Schedule a five-minute mindfulness meditation three times per week.

Step 3: Introduce the concept of meditation with this video for children aged 7–12 as an example of how to manage frustration by simply changing your thoughts: schools.au.reachout.com/wellbeing-5s/i-woke-up-early-on-the-weekend-meditation

Step 4: Test out a silent meditation at home before practising with your students. This way you can relate to the experience and understand how they may feel at the beginning of the process.

Step 5: Encourage your students to sit comfortably and quietly with their eyes lowered or closed. Use a timer and ensure adequate space between students. Expand from one to five minutes over time and praise their progress. Experiment with peaceful indoor and outdoor locations.

During a mindfulness meditation, encourage children to sit comfortably and quietly with lowered or closed eyes

CHAPTER 8

Conclusion

This Wellbeing handbook is a starting point for educators committed to embracing new initiatives, large or small, to nurture students socially and emotionally, with the goal of making schools a regenerative space for educators and the whole school community. A wellbeing project will take time and resources, but the rewards for educators and students are incredibly worthwhile.

Ideally the concepts, case studies, tips and activities suggested in this book will help you, the educator, to inspire others to join a gentle movement towards less abrasive, more sensitive practices in schools – to bring out the best in your students. Little by little, the small things will add up to something that students will remember for life!

A school community with a sense of wellbeing allows learning to flourish in a safe setting, where every child's emotional vulnerabilities are recognized and respected, along with the needs of their educators. As an early adopter of a wellbeing initiative in your classroom, you are planting a seed and gently encouraging an educational ecosystem to grow into a fertile jungle, teaming with life and learning.

By taking care of ourselves – socially and emotionally – we can authentically lead by example and have a greater impact on the children we are entrusted with and whom we are honoured to work with. In this handbook, my aim was to share the recipe for creating a calm and collaborative classroom, filled with happy, high-achieving students and educators. Reflecting on the 'How to help' sections, I know there is potential for students to feel impacted by educators who care enough to listen and find solutions.

Working together

The wellbeing of educators is essential to fostering a classroom where student wellbeing is also prioritized. Take time to connect with your colleagues and to write to me (**kimberley@quirkykid.com.au**) to let me know how your wellbeing initiatives are taking shape. Going beyond the clinical setting to help students on a broader scale in a global context is high on my list of priorities. A tiny flower in a teeny glass may be your first and most important step in this process!

It is easy to feel overwhelmed as a professional working with children when we are incredibly committed to resolving issues and nurturing the potential in every young person. The case studies used in this book are likely to reflect many of the students in your classes and on my client load, but by continuing to embrace the challenge, it has become evident that the little things do matter in the greater scheme of things.

We are valuing our humanity by encouraging students to take a stretch in the sun, to go barefoot, or to pick some flowers for the classroom. By prioritizing cognitive stimulation as an important aspect of wellbeing, we are ensuring that students have new materials to absorb – new sights, sounds, textures and tastes to consume. Think of yourself as a gourmet traveller, exploring new, exotic locations and indulging your senses. You are the guide and your students are your curious entourage.

IB Learner Profile

By taking the time to explore the 10 behaviours of the learner profile at the heart of the PYP in detail, educators are asked to consciously bring each profile into the classroom on a regular basis, to help students identify with them. By understanding how to strengthen your personal capacity to be more 'balanced' or 'principled', students learn where to focus their attention.

To inspire educators with ways to build capacity in every IB Learner Profile attribute, activities have been suggested. One of the key learnings is to model these behaviours in your work. Be curious, be knowledgeable and be principled in your teaching methods. Another key learning is to put yourself in your student's position. For those students who are not natural communicators, ask yourself, 'What would it be like to sit silently in a discussion, wishing you had the confidence to contribute?' Remember why it is necessary to enhance every one of those IB Learner Profile attributes – they are important life skills and, without them, students will experience their own limitations and frustrations.

Let students lead

Students, too, can be role models for each other by striving for greatness and bringing out the best in themselves and others. Consistently treating others with respect is an important aspect of great leadership. There are many examples in this book where I have suggested giving students roles and responsibilities. Having a long list of special jobs, like raising the school flag, offering tech support at assembly, collecting eggs, jumping on cardboard boxes, driving a wheelbarrow or recording what items are in the lost and found basket, are all important roles – give them freely for best results!

Giving students with less social status leadership roles is a great way to affirm the value of differences. Just as having your racial identity affirmed by an educator is scientifically proven to increase academic achievement (Ladson-Billings, 2009; Wright et al., 2015), students respond to feeling valued. Being given a special role or responsibility also increases students' sense of belonging at school – it provides structure for students who like to know where they are needed.

Teaching empathy, compassion and respect starts with an emotional investment in each individual student and the time required to foster a connection. This will vary depending on the student and their own personal circumstances. Trust is a key component in every teacher–student relationship. As an educator, you will influence young people, even if they keep their distance. Your actions will be observed by those around you. Consistency makes it easier for your students to follow your lead.

Go easy on yourself

No one learns without making mistakes (Guzman Ingram, 2017). Educators who persevere acknowledge the challenges of failure and the energy required to push through uncertainty. Taking care of yourself is influenced by the daily decisions we make about what time we go to bed, what we eat for dinner and our willingness to commit to doing sport or attending social opportunities!

At the end of a working week, those decisions may amount to feeling satisfied or depleted, depending on the social, emotional and physical benefits of each decision. Choose wisely, but start afresh with every new opportunity to make a choice. Feeling guilty about a decision you made last week will not change it. Being mindful that children are more likely to adopt a balanced lifestyle when educators and parents promote similar values may help you to go easy on yourself and start over.

To be reflective, we must process information and evaluate it. Being reflective is about considering our own strengths and weaknesses as professionals committed to our work with young people, and as leaders in the field of student wellbeing. This helps us to know where we need to improve and how we can better contribute in the future as champions of change.

LEARNER PROFILE WORKSHEETS

Inquirers

> We nurture our curiosity, developing skills for inquiry and research. We know how to learn independently and with others. We learn with enthusiasm and sustain our love of learning throughout life.

Complete this activity to think like an Inquirer!

Step 1: Look at the matchbox your teacher is holding up.

Learner Profile worksheets: Inquirers

Step 2: Go on a scavenger hunt and find **five** tiny items in the playground that will all fit into the matchbox. It could be seeds, stones or other interesting items.

Step 3: In the classroom, line up your items and study each one closely. Use a magnifying glass if you have one.

Step 4: Choose one item and draw it, or create a story about it.

Step 5: Walk carefully around your classroom and study all the items, slowly and closely. Think about everyday objects in familiar places and how valuable and intriguing they might be!

LEARNER PROFILE WORKSHEETS

Knowledgeable

We develop and use conceptual understanding, exploring knowledge across a range of disciplines. We engage with issues and ideas that have local and global significance.

Step 1: In groups, choose a topic that is important in the world today – for example, water use, recycling, animal rights, transport or food.

Learner Profile worksheets: Knowledgeable

Step 2: Draw something from your local area that is related to your chosen topic. For example, if you chose *food*, you could draw what you eat at home.

Step 3: Use your research skills and choose another part of the world as a different context in which to research your topic. For example, with food, you could draw popular dishes or foods from that region, and place the picture on the right part of a map.

Step 4: Discuss these questions in groups:

- What do students around the world have in common?
- What differences did you discover in regard to your topic?
- What other questions did your research raise?

Discover the answers to your questions.

Share your new knowledge with your classmates.

LEARNER PROFILE WORKSHEETS

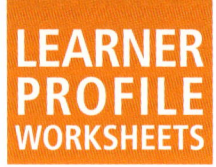

Thinkers

We use critical and creative thinking skills to analyse and take responsible action on complex problems. We exercise initiative in making reasoned, ethical decisions.

Step 1: Have you ever noticed a problem that needs fixing? I bet you have plenty of ideas!

Draw or write about the problem you discovered.

Learner Profile worksheets: Thinkers

Step 2: Can you break the problem into smaller pieces? This will help you to solve it in parts, one step at a time.

For example, a garbage bin that is overflowing may have three parts to it:

1 Too much garbage	2 No one to empty bin	3 Garbage blowing into a river or ocean

Step 3: Draw or write about three different parts of the problem you discovered.

Can you find a solution for each small part of the problem? For example:

1 Too much garbage	2 No one to empty bin	3 Garbage blowing into a river or ocean
Solution: Reduce the amount of waste or add an extra bin.	Solution: Volunteer to empty the bin more frequently or find someone who can.	Solution: Put a lid on the garbage bin and pull the waste from the water.

Use the table on the next page to break your problem into smaller pieces and to find solutions for each part.

Learner Profile worksheets: Thinkers

1	2	3
Solution:	Solution:	Solution:

LEARNER PROFILE WORKSHEETS

Communicators

We express ourselves confidently and creatively in more than one language and in many ways. We collaborate effectively, listening carefully to the perspective of other individuals and groups.

Is it easier to listen/talk to someone if they are facing towards you or away from you?

Step 1: Find a partner, move to an open space and sit back to back.

Step 2: Take turns to talk and listen for 30 seconds each. One person talks, the other listens, and then you should switch roles. You should both have a turn to talk and listen.

Learner Profile worksheets: Communicators

Step 3: Turn around and face each other and try the same thing again. This time the listener can see the talker's eyes, hands and facial expressions. Swap over after 30 seconds so you both have a turn to talk and listen again.

Step 4: Answer these questions together:

- Was it easier for you to listen when you were facing away from each other or sitting face to face? Why do you think this was the case?

- Was it easier to talk when you were facing away from each other or sitting face to face? Why do you think this was the case?

Step 5: Take a class vote and see how many of your classmates preferred facing away and how many preferred sitting face to face when communicating. Together, discuss the reasons why.

LEARNER PROFILE WORKSHEETS

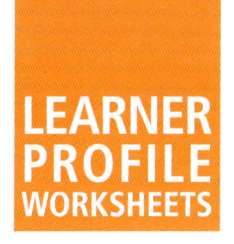

Principled

We act with integrity and honesty, with a strong sense of fairness and justice and with respect for the dignity and rights of people everywhere. We take responsibility for our actions and their consequences.

Step 1: Consider the phrase:

'Be the change you want to see in the world.'
Mahatma Gandhi

Step 2: Imagine you were selected to lead your country. As a leader with a strong sense of fairness, what changes would you like to implement? Make a list. Think about how these changes might affect the rights of people everywhere.

Learner Profile worksheets: Principled

Step 3: How would you put these changes into practice?

Write about, or draw a picture, showing how you could be the change you want to see in the world.

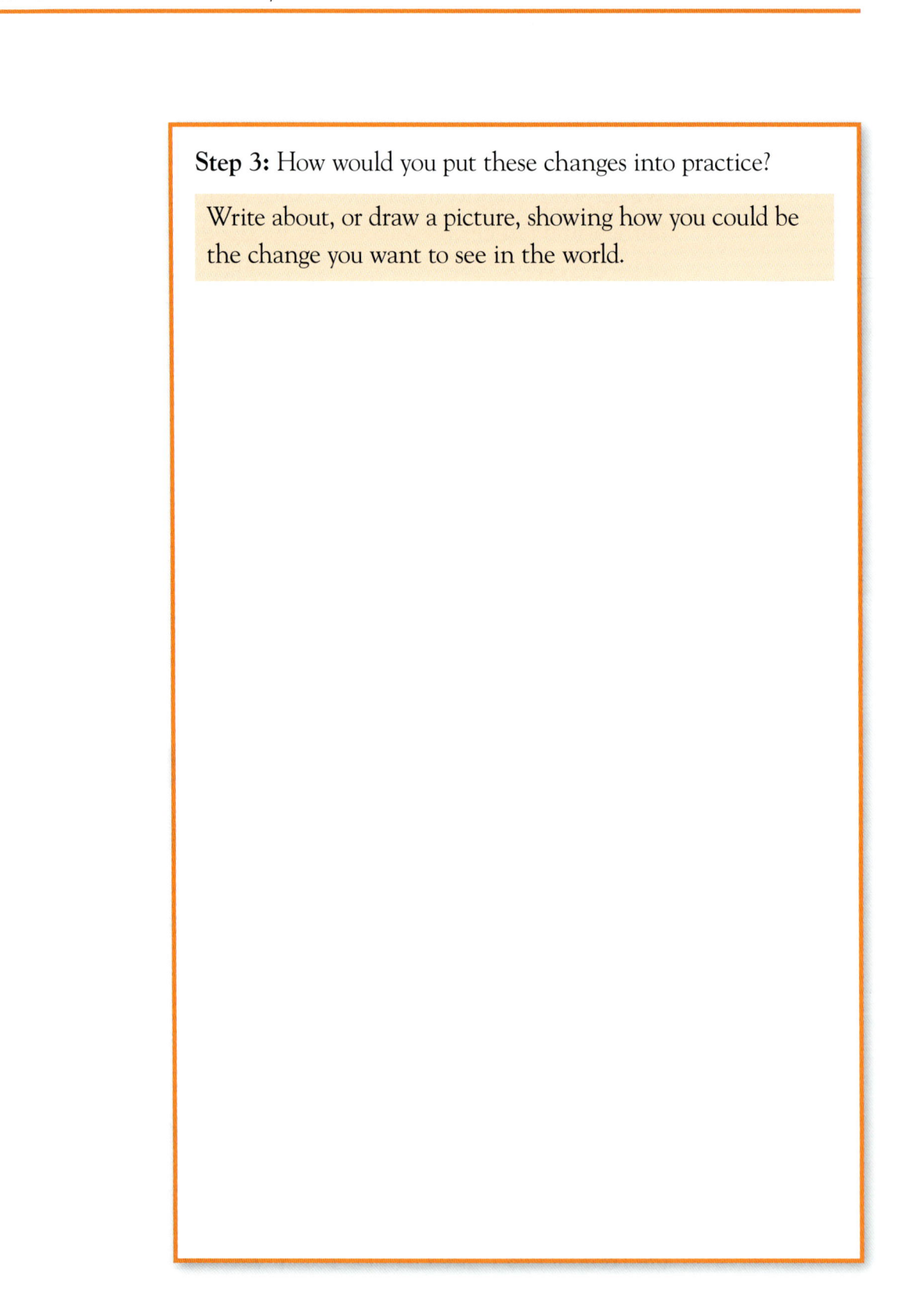

LEARNER PROFILE WORKSHEETS

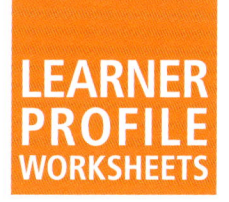

Open-minded

> We critically appreciate our own cultures and personal histories, as well as the values and traditions of others. We seek and evaluate a range of points of view, and we are willing to grow from the experience.

Step 1: Design a survey to find out different perspectives from other students at your school. Choose a topic that will likely have different points of view, and use a scale for each question, such as the one shown below.

Strongly disagree	Disagree	Undecided	Agree	Strongly agree
1	2	3	4	5

Step 2: Try to survey as many students as possible! Your teacher will tell you how long you have to complete your surveys.

Step 3: When your surveys are complete, have a look at the responses. Find the question in the survey that has the most diverse range of responses, ie a mix of 5s and 1s.

Step 4: Consider the different points of view on this particular question. Why do you think the responses were so diverse? Share your question and thoughts with the rest of the class.

LEARNER PROFILE WORKSHEETS

Caring

We show empathy, compassion and respect. We have a commitment to service, and we act to make a positive difference in the lives of others and in the world around us.

Step 1: List ideas that would be helpful to, or appreciated by others.

Step 2: Your teacher will set up a reward system for your class, like a marble jar. Each time you or somebody in your class completes a random act of kindness, you will be one step closer to your class reward!

Step 3: Once you have reached your reward for random acts of kindness, brainstorm places where you should focus your next set of random acts of kindness – for example, in the classroom, in the playground or in the canteen.

LEARNER PROFILE WORKSHEETS

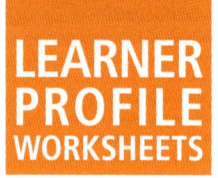

Risk-takers

> We approach uncertainty with forethought and determination. We work independently and cooperatively to explore new ideas and innovative strategies. We are resourceful and resilient in the face of challenges and change.

Step 1: Think about the power of 'yet' – 'I can't do this *yet*' rather than 'I can't do this'.

Step 2: Your teacher is going to set you a challenge that is slightly more difficult than your regular classwork.

Step 3: You teacher will record how you find the challenge.

Step 4: Your teacher will set a timer for two minutes and ask you to *persevere*. Self-reflect on any challenges you faced when trying to persevere and how difficult you found the challenge. You could share thoughts with your peers if you want to.

Learner Profile worksheets: Risk-takers

> **Step 5:** Celebrate your perseverance and the progress you have made as a class. Your teacher will set you a daily or weekly challenge to practise your risk-taking skills. Rate your own risk-taking as learners for each task:
>
> ✔ 40 = 'I can't do this *yet*'
>
> ✔ 0 = 'I can't do this'

Use your self-ratings to make a graph at the end of the challenging set task. See the example below.

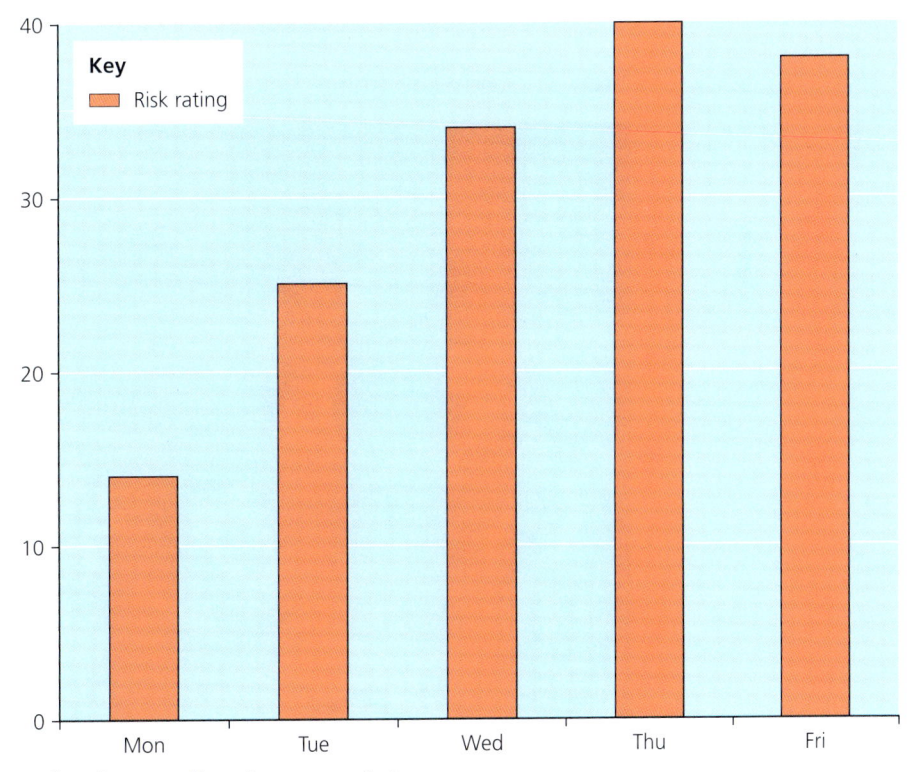

Risk-taker's self-rating – week 1

LEARNER PROFILE WORKSHEETS

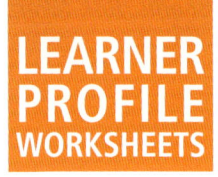

Balanced

We understand the importance of balancing different aspects of our lives – intellectual, physical and emotional – to achieve wellbeing for ourselves and others. We recognize our interdependence with other people and with the world in which we live.

Step 1: Your teacher will explain *interdependence* to you. Discuss your understanding of the word with a partner.

Step 2: Study the image below.

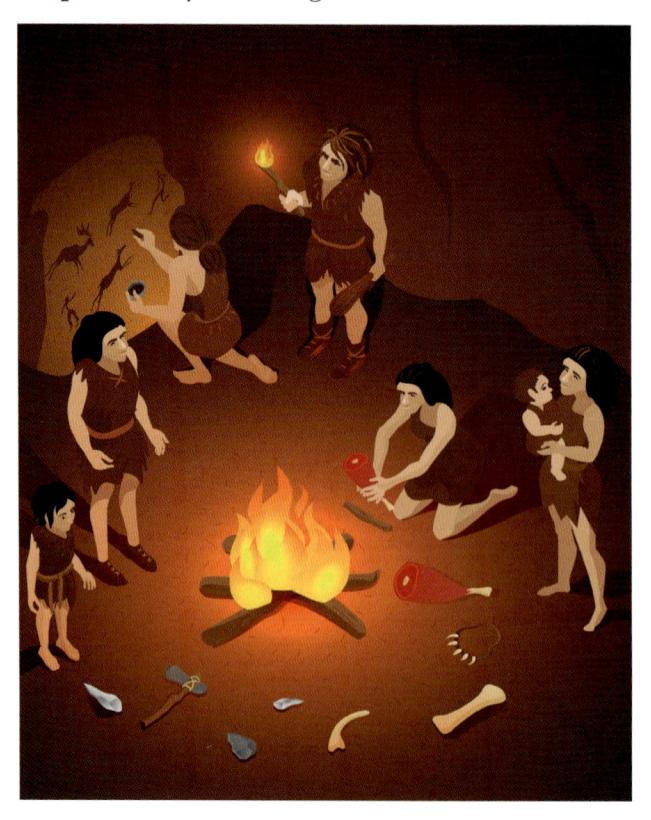

This is a family of hunters and gatherers. At night, the fire was a place to keep warm and listen to stories. By day, some hunted and others gathered food to survive. The children collected firewood, and helped to carry water and keep the babies safe.

Why do you think hunters and gatherers did not live alone? List three ideas.

1 ....

2 ....

3 ....

Step 3: Study the image below.

SOCIETY

This is a modern community. There are many different jobs in today's human society, compared to the hunter gatherers. There are teachers, firefighters, shop assistants – all kinds of jobs! In many households, children help to cook dinner, keep the house tidy and go to school.

Learner Profile worksheets: Balanced

Do you think we still need to live together in today's society? Why or why not?

....

....

....

Step 4: Study the image below.

This is an image of a woman who is dressed up and her hair is neat, suggesting she may be going to meet someone (socially). She is doing exercise by riding her scooter to take care of herself (physically) and her facial expression appears calm (emotionally). She appears *balanced* – socially, emotionally and physically.

Learner Profile worksheets: Balanced

Step 5: On each circle below, write 'socially', 'emotionally' and 'physically' in each circle. Think about your routine and draw or write, in each circle, what you do to keep yourself balanced and how you take care of yourself – socially, emotionally and physically.

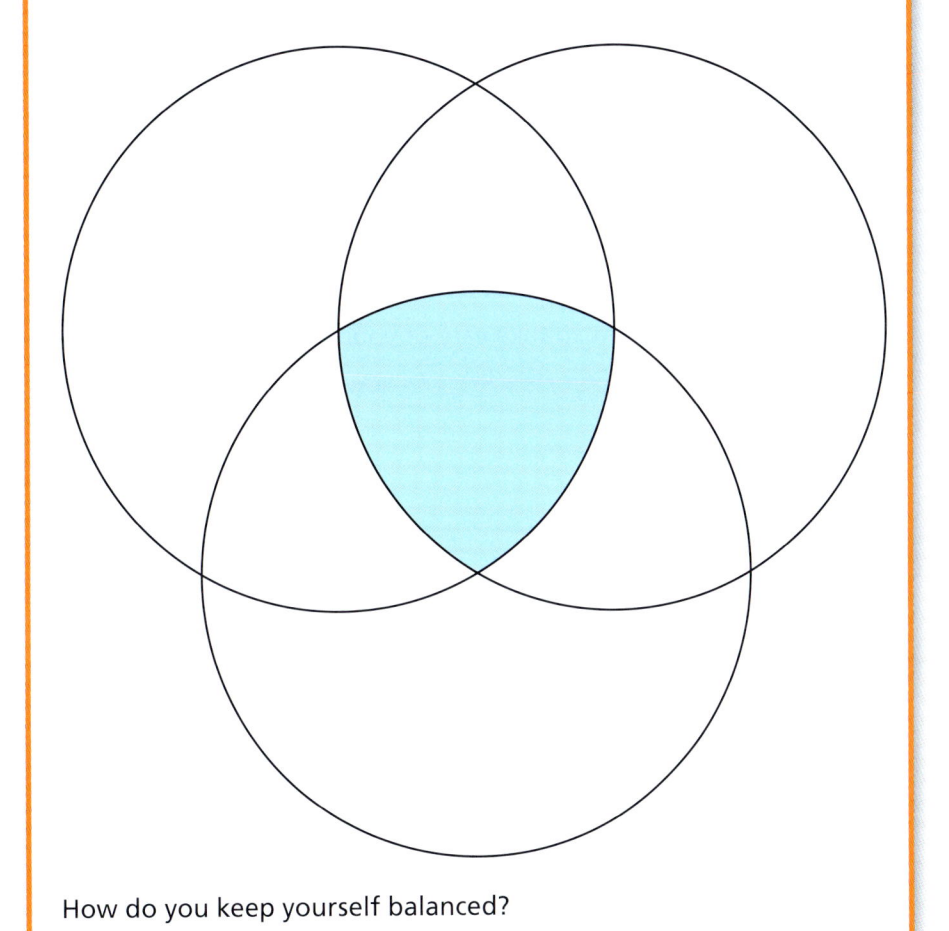

How do you keep yourself balanced?

Learner Profile worksheets: Balanced

Step 6: Share your ideas in a small group and discuss the ideas below.

Socially	Physically	Emotionally
☑ Go to a playground	☑ Walk up stairs	☑ Hug yourself
☑ Invite a friend over	☑ Run home	☑ Pat an animal
☑ Share something	☑ Ride a bike	☑ Put flowers in a vase
☑ Post a surprise	☑ Join a team sport	☑ Get nice and clean
☑ Visit a neighbour	☑ Skip with a rope	☑ Take a big stretch
☑ Plan a little party	☑ Do sit-ups	☑ Write in a journal

How to take care of yourself

LEARNER PROFILE WORKSHEETS

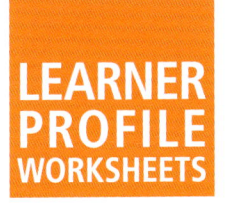

Reflective

We thoughtfully consider the world and our own ideas and experience. We work to understand our strengths and weaknesses in order to support our learning and personal development.

Step 1: Think about all the textures in the world around you. Look around your classroom and touch all the different textures you can find. Can you touch something soft, rough, jagged or fluffy? What other textures can you find?

Step 2: Now look outside your classroom, around the school grounds, to seek out even more different textures. Collect a diverse range of samples of textures and stick them in your journal.

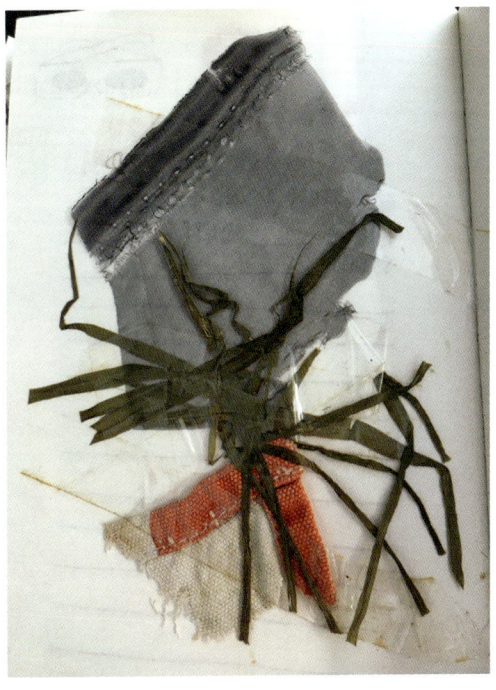

Photograph of journal item courtesy of Olivia Rocker (aged 12)

109

Learner Profile worksheets: Reflective

Step 3: Consider your own strengths and weaknesses as textures. Some parts of ourselves may be solid and strong, for example. These are our strengths. Other parts may be soft and fragile. These are our weaknesses. Using the different textures you have found, craft a sculpture or symbol of yourself.

You could either:

a Stick the textures in a journal in the form of yourself, labelling your own strengths and weaknesses.

b Create a sculpture of yourself using the textures and write a sentence about how it is like you.

Here is an example:

'I am balanced most of the time, but if I tip over I'm still learning how to fix things myself.'

Creating a sculpture using different textures

Step 4: Reflect on this activity in a class discussion. Answer these questions:

- How did it feel to collect the different textures?

- How did it feel to consider your own strengths and weaknesses?

- How did you feel about creating an image of yourself with the textures?

BIBLIOGRAPHY

Asher, SR and Paquette, J. 2003. 'Loneliness and peer relations in childhood'. *Current Directions in Psychological Science*, *12*, 75–8.

Barblett, L and Maloney, C. 2010. 'Complexities of assessing social and emotional competence and wellbeing in young children'. *Australasian Journal of Early Childhood*, *35*(2), 13–18.

Barlow, FK, Louis, WR and Hewstone, M. 2009. 'Rejected! Cognitions of rejection and intergroup anxiety as mediators of the impact of cross-group friendships on prejudice'. *British Journal of Social Psychology*, *48*, 389–405.

Berto, R and Barbiero, G. 2014. 'Mindful silence produces long lasting attentional performance in children'. *Visions for Sustainability*, *2*, 49–60.

Boe, EE, Cook, LH and Sunderland, RJ. 2008. 'Teacher Turnover: Examining Exit Attrition, Teaching Area Transfer, and School Migration'. *Exceptional Children*, *75*, 7-31.

Brussoni, M, Gibbons, R, Gray, C, Ishikawa, T, Sandseter, E, Bienenstock, A, Chabot, G, *et al*. 2015. 'What is the relationship between risky outdoor play and health in children? A systematic review'. *International Journal of Environmental Research and Public Health*, *12*(6), 6423–54.

Cacioppo, S, Grippo, AJ, London, S, Goossens, L and Cacioppo, JT. 2015. 'Loneliness: Clinical import and interventions'. *Perspectives on Psychological Science*, *10*, 238–49.

Chouinard, MM. 2007. 'Children's questions: A mechanism for cognitive development'. *Monographs of the Society for Research in Child Development*, *72*, 45–57.

Christensen, TM and Thorngren, JM. 2000. 'Integrating play in family therapy: An interview with Eliana Gil, Ph.D'. *The Family Journal*, *8*(1), 91–100.

Cooker, L, Bailey, L, Stevenson, H and Joseph, S. 2016. *Social and Emotional Well-Being in IB World Schools: Ages 3–19*. Washington, DC. International Baccalaureate Organization. Retrieved from **https://www.ibo.org/contentassets/318968269ae5441d8df5ae76542817a0/research-continuum-social-and-emotional-well-being-in-ib-world-school-final-report.pdf**

Dempsey, A, Sulkowski, M, Nichols, R and Storch, E. 2009. 'Differences between peer victimization in cyber and physical settings and associated psychosocial adjustment in early adolescence'. *Psychology in the Schools*, *46*(10), 962–72.

Dornan, J. 2004. *Blood From the Moon: Gender Ideology and the Rise of Ancient Maya Social Complexity. Gender and History*. New York. Oxford University Press.

Durlak, JA, Domitrovich, CE, Weissberg, RP and Gullotta, TP, (eds). 2015. *Handbook of Social and Emotional learning: Research and Practice*. New York. Guilford Press.

Dweck, C. 2006. *Mindset: The New Psychology of Success*. New York. Ballantine Books.

Education Support. 2019. *Teacher Wellbeing Index 2019*. London. Education Support. Retrieved from **www.educationsupport.org.uk/resources/research-reports/teacher-wellbeing-index-2019**

Eisenberger, NI, Lieberman, MD and Williams, KD. 2003. 'The pains and pleasure of social life: A social cognitive neuroscience approach'. *Science*, *302*, 290–311.

Fantz, RL. 1964. 'Visual experience in infants: Decrease attention to familiar patterns relative to novel ones'. *Science*, *146*(3644), 668–70.

Felver, JC, Tipsord, JM, Morris, MJ, Racer, KH and Dishion, TJ. 2017. 'The effects of mindfulness-based intervention on children's attention regulation'. *Journal of Attention Disorders*, *21*(10), 872–81.

Flook, L, Smalley, S, Kitil, MJ, Galla, BM, Kaiser-Greenland, S, Locke, J, Ishijima, E and Kasari, C. 2010. 'Effects of mindful awareness practices on executive functions in elementary school children'. *Journal of Applied School Psychology*, *26*(1), 70–95.

Fontaine, R, Yang, C, Burks, V, Dodge, K, Price, J and Pettit, G. 2009. 'Loneliness as a partial mediator of the relation between low social preference in childhood and anxious/depressed symptoms in adolescence'. *Development and Psychopathology*, *21*, 479–91.

Giannetti, CC and Sagarese, M. 2001. 'Does your child click with a clique? Help your child uncover the truth about cliques and belonging'. *Our Children*, *26*(6), 9–10.

Gluckman, P. 2011. *Improving the Transition: Reducing Social and Psychological Morbidity During Adolescence*. A report for the Prime Minister's Chief Science Advisor. Auckland. Office of the Prime Minister's Science Advisory Committee.

Guzman Ingram, L. 2017. 'A classroom full of risk takers'. *Edutopia*. Retrieved from www.edutopia.org/article/classroom-full-risk-takers

Hausmann, LRM, Ye, F, Schofield, JW and Woods, RL. 2009. 'Sense of belonging and persistence in white and African American first-year students'. *Research in Higher Education*, *50*, 649–69.

Heaven, PCL, Ciarrochi, J and Vialle, W. 2008. 'Self-nominated peer crowds, school achievement, and psychological adjustment in adolescents: Longitudinal analysis'. *Personality and Individual Differences*, *44*, 977–88.

International Baccalaureate Organization. 2017. *What Is an IB Education?* Retrieved from www.ibo.org/

Keigher, A and Cross, F. 2010. 'Teacher Attrition and Mobility: Results from the 2008-2009 Teacher Follow-Up Survey'. Washington, D.C. National Center for Education Statistics (NCES 2010-353).

Koenig, L, Isaacs, A and Schwartz, J. 1994. 'Gender differences in adolescent depression and loneliness: Why are boys lonelier if girls are more depressed?' *Journal of Research in Personality*, *28*, 27–43.

Kounios, J and Beeman, M. 2009. 'The Aha! moment: The cognitive neuroscience of insight'. *Current Directions in Psychological Science*, *18*(4), 210–16.

Ladson-Billings, G. 2009. *The Dreamkeepers: Successful Teachers of African-American Children*, 2nd ed. San Francisco. Jossey-Bass.

Landy, FJ and Conte, JM. 2013. *Work in the 21st century: An Introduction to Industrial and Organizational Psychology (4th Ed.)*. John Wiley & Sons, Inc.

Lasgaard, M, Goossens, L and Elklit, A. 2011. 'Loneliness, depressive symptomatology, and suicide ideation in adolescence: Cross-sectional and longitudinal analyses'. *Journal of Abnormal Child Psychology*, *39*(1), 137–50.

Levant, R and Kopecky, G. 1995. *Masculinity Reconstructed: Changing the Rules of Manhood – at Work, in Relationships, and in Family Life*. New York. Dutton.

Lindqvist, P, Nordanger, U and Carlsson, R. 2014. 'Teacher attrition the first five years – A multifaceted image'. *Teaching and Teacher Education*, *40*, 94–103.

Mahoney, J, Durlak, J and Weissberg, R. 2018. 'An update on social and emotional learning outcome research'. *Phi Delta Kappan*, *100*, 18–23.

Malcolm, E, Evans-Lacko, S, Little, K, Henderson, C and Thornicroft, G. 2013. 'The impact of exercise projects to promote mental wellbeing'. *Journal of Mental Health*, *22*(6), 519–27.

Neilsen-Hewett, C. 2001. *Children's Peer Relations and School Adjustment: Looking Beyond the Classroom Walls*. Doctoral dissertation, Macquarie University, Sydney.

Noble, T, McGrath, H, Roffey, S and Rowling, L. 2008. *A Scoping Study on Student Well-Being*. Canberra, ACT. Department of Education, Employment & Workplace Relations.

Nishina, A, Juvonen, J and Witkow, M. 2005. 'Sticks and stones may break my bones, but names will make me feel sick: The psychosocial, somatic, and scholastic consequences of peer harassment'. *Journal of Clinical Child and Adolescent Psychology*, *34*, 37–48.

Oberle, E, Schonert-Reichl, KA and Zumbo, BD. 2011. 'Life satisfaction in early adolescence: Personal, neighborhood, school, family, and peer influences'. *Journal of Youth and Adolescence*, *40*(7), 889–901.

O'Brien, KM. 2017. *Belonging and Socioemotional Wellbeing Among Students in Transition from Primary to Secondary School*. Figshare. Thesis, Monash University, Melbourne. Retrieved from doi.org/10.4225/03/58b8a577c41df

Bibliography

OECD. 2019. *TALIS 2018 Results (Volume I): Teachers and School Leaders as Lifelong Learners.* Paris. OECD Publishing.

Parker, JG and Asher, S. 1993. 'Friendship and friendship quality in middle childhood: Links with peer group acceptance and feelings of loneliness'. *Developmental Psychology*, 29, 611–21.

Pellegrini, AD and Long, JD. 2002. 'The longitudinal study of bullying, dominance, and victimization during the transition from primary school through secondary school'. *British Journal of Developmental Psychology*, 20, 259–80.

Purser, R. 2019. *McMindfulness: How Mindfulness Became the New Capitalist Spirituality.* London. Repeater Books.

Rabi, II. 1960. *My Life and Times as a Physicist.* Claremont, CA. Claremont College.

Rapee, R. 2012. 'Anxiety disorders in children and adolescents: Nature, development, treatment and prevention'. *The International Association for Child and Adolescent Psychiatry and Allied Professionals Textbook of Child and Adolescent Mental Health*, section F.1, pp. 1–19.

Roffey, S. 2019. *Creative Caring for Teachers: How a Whole-School Well-Being Approach Can Support Everyone's Mental Health.* EdCan. Retrieved from www.edcan.ca/articles/creative-caring-teachers/

Rubin, K, Coplan, R and Bowker, J. 2009. 'Social withdrawal in childhood'. *Annual Review of Psychology*, 60, 141–71.

Sanders, J. 2019. *Hey There! What's Your Superpower?: A Book to Encourage a Growth Mindset of Resilience, Persistence, Self-Confidence, Self-Reliance and Self-Esteem.* Victoria. Educate2Empower Publishing.

Sheinman, N, Hadar, L, Gafni, L and Milman, D. 2018. 'Preliminary investigation of whole-school mindfulness in education programs and children's mindfulness-based coping strategies'. *Journal of Child and Family Studies*, 27, 3316–28.

Shute, R, De Blasio, T and Williamson, P. 2002. 'Social support satisfaction of Australian children'. *International Journal of Behavioural Development*, 26(4), 318–26.

Siu, AMH. 2019. 'Self-harm and suicide among children and adolescents in Hong Kong: A review of prevalence, risk factors, and prevention strategies'. *Journal of Adolescent Health*, 64(6), S59–64.

Stegar, MF and Kashdan, TB. 2009. 'Depression and everyday social activity, belonging and well-being'. *Journal of Counselling Psychology*, 56(2), 289–300.

Taylor, RD, Oberle, E, Durlak, JA and Weissberg, RP. 2017. 'Promoting positive youth development through school-based social and emotional learning interventions: A meta-analysis of follow-up effects'. *Child Development*, 88(4), 1156–71.

UNICEF Mongolia. 2012. *Teachers in Mongolia: An Empirical Study on Recruitment into Teaching, Professional Development, and Retention of Teachers.* Ulaanbaatar. UNICEF Mongolia.

Van Cuylenburg, H. 2019. *The Resilience Project: Finding Happiness Through Gratitude, Empathy & Mindfulness.* Melbourne. Penguin Random House.

Walton, GM and Cohen, GL. 2007. 'A question of belonging: Race, social fit, and achievement'. *Journal of Personality and Social Psychology*, 92(1), 82–96. doi.org/10.1037/0022-3514.92.1.82

Weissberg, RP. 2019. 'Promoting the social and emotional learning of millions of school children'. *Perspectives on Psychological Science*, 14(1), 65–9.

Wellbeing. 2019. In *Oxford Online Dictionary.* Retrieved from https://www.lexico.com/definition/well-being

Williams, KD. 2009. *Advances in Experimental Social Psychology.* San Diego, CA. Academic Press.

Witvliet, M, Brendgen, M, van Lier, PAC, Koot, HM and Vitaro, F. 2010. 'Early adolescent depressive symptoms: Prediction from clique isolation, loneliness, and perceived social acceptance'. *Journal of Abnormal Child Psychology*, 38(8), 1045–56.

Wright, BL, Counsell, SL and Tate, SL. 2015. '"We're many members, but one body". Fostering a healthy self-identity and agency in African-American boys'. *Young Children*, 70(3), 24–31.

INDEX

A
academic achievement 1, 8, 57, 78–9, 87
advocating 50–1
aggressive behaviour 46
anger management 46
anxiety 69, 75–81
   signs of 77, 79
anxiety disorders 77
anxiety management 78–81
   see also mindfulness
Approaches to Learning (ATL) skills 40–4
   communication skills 56–64
   self-management skills 65–74
   social skills 45–55
audio information streams 61
avoidance behaviours 66, 77–9

B
babies 19
Balanced approach 17, 32–6, 104–8
behavioural changes 77
belonging 13, 41, 56, 87
blankets, weighted lap 66
bodily sensations, awareness of 81
body language 42, 55, 56, 61, 96
Buehner, Carl W. 4

C
calm spaces 66
'capturing the moment' 74
caring approach 17, 28–9, 100–1
cartoons 67–8
case studies
   anxiety and avoidance behaviours 78–9
   inconsistent friendships 52–3
   interpreting 60
   listening skills 57
   loud leadership 49
   meltdowns 66
   mindfulness meditation 82
   perseverance 69
   problems in the playground 46
   resilience 72–3
   tongue tied children 63
challenges 30–1, 57, 68, 70–1, 73, 102–3
charitable causes 28
China 8
classrooms
   environment 6
   participation 12–13, 21, 57
   Primary Years Programme 4–9
   strategies for implementing wellbeing in 10–12
closed-mindedness 26
cognitive stimulation 32
Cohen, GL 40
collaboration 7, 24–5, 45–51, 85–6, 95
comfort zones, stepping outside 30
communication skills 56–64
   and gender stereotypes 43
   interpreting 56, 60–4
   listening 24–5, 56–9, 96
   speaking 56, 63–4, 96
   and wellbeing 42–3
Communicators 17, 18, 24–5, 95–6
compassion 28–9, 87, 100
consensus 50
control, children's lack of 4
Cuba 2
culture 60–1
curiosity 19–20, 88
curriculum 8

D
depressive symptoms 41
dominant children 49

E
effort 31
emails 12, 60, 66, 69, 73, 78–9
emotional intelligence 51–5
emotional needs 32–6
emotional regulation 8–9, 44, 54, 65, 66–8
emotional triggers 66–8, 77–9
emotional wellbeing 1–2, 6–9, 13, 18, 106–8
emotionally reactive children 72–3
emotions 77
   mapping 55
empathy 28–9, 47–8, 87, 100
exams, outdoor 8

F
failure
   fear of 69
   learning through 30, 31, 87
fairness 25–6, 97–8
food options, healthy 32
friendships 41–2, 60
   as source of stress 45, 52–3

G
Gandhi, Mahatma 26, 97
gender differences 42
gender stereotypes 43
Ghana 1–2
Gil, Eliana 24
global, the 21–2
groups 41, 49, 55
   discussions 22
growth mindsets 22

H
health 32, 40, 75, 77
   see also mental health
helping others 28–9
high achievers 57
humour, sense of 1
hunters and gatherers 33–4, 104–5

I
IB *see* International Baccalaureate
ideas, clear expression 63–4
impulsivity 49
independence, inspiring 19
information streams 61
Inquirers 17, 18, 19–20, 88–9
Insight Timer 81
integrity 25–6, 97
intelligence
   emotional 51–5
   social 51–5
intelligence quotient (IQ) 20
interdependence 32–6, 104–5
International Baccalaureate (IB) 2
   curriculum 8
   Diploma Programme (DP) 6
   Middle Years Programme (MYP) 6
   Primary Years Programme (PYP) 4–9, 16
   and teamwork 7
International Baccalaureate (IB) Leaner Profiles
   overview 17
   and wellbeing 16–39, 86
   worksheets 88–111
interpreting 56, 60–4

J
justice 25–6, 97

K
kindness, acts of random 29, 100–1
Knowledgeable approach 17, 18, 20–2, 90–1

L
leadership
   loud 49
   Principled 25–6
   providing opportunities for 86–7
Leaner Profiles *see* International Baccalaureate (IB) Leaner Profiles
learning
   lifelong 19
   social and emotional (SEL) 2, 4–15
   through failure 30, 31, 87
   see also Approaches to Learning (ATL) skills
learning behaviours, practical strategies to foster 16, 18–39
lifelong learning 19
listening skills 24–5, 56–9, 96
Listening Tours 58–9
local, the 21–2
loneliness 40, 41
loud children 49, 58

M
McBrearty, Sinéad 5
marble jar reward system 29, 100–1
meditation, mindfulness 81–4
meltdowns 66
mental health 41

index

mind maps 63
mindfulness 75, 81–4
mindsets, growth 22
mistakes, learning through 30, 31, 87

N
National Children's Bureau 14
nature-based resources 55
needs 32–6

O
occupational therapists 66
Open-mindedness 17, 18, 26–8, 99
oral information streams 61
Organisation for Economic Co-operation and Development (OECD) 76
overwhelm 85–6
oxytocin 5

P
participation, classroom 12–13, 21, 57
performance pressure 78–9
perseverance 30–1, 43, 65, 68–71, 102–3
personal strengths/weaknesses 37–8, 109–11
perspective-taking 9, 47–8, 99
physical exercise 4–5, 32
physical health 32, 40, 75, 77
physical needs 32–6
physical wellbeing 4–5, 6, 106–8
play-based activities 24
playground problems 46–8
power imbalances 50
Principled approach 17, 18, 25–6, 97–8
problem-solving skills 22–3, 92–4
Purser, Ronald 82

Q
Quirky Kid® Clinic 3, 76

R
Rabi, Isidor 19
Reflective approaches 17, 18, 36–8, 87, 109–11
relationships 2, 8, 13

relaxation strategies 79, 80–1
relevance 21–2
resilience 30–1, 65, 71–4, 102
respect 28, 86, 87, 97, 100
responsibilities 12, 13, 22, 30, 47, 52, 57, 67, 72, 86–7
reward systems, marble jar 29, 100–1
Risk-takers 17, 18, 30–1, 70, 102–3
Rocker, Leonardo 3
role-modelling 8–9, 19, 25, 86–7
role-playing 46
roles 12, 13, 22, 47, 52, 57, 67, 72, 86–7
rules, confusion regarding 46

S
safety issues 6
sand play 24
school leaders, role of 6–7
SEL see social and emotional learning
self-awareness 8–9, 26, 81
self-care 107–8
self-confidence 30
self-criticism 87
self-esteem 21, 63
self-expression 24–5
self-management skills 65–74
    definition 65
    emotional regulation 8–9, 44, 54, 65, 66–8
    and wellbeing 43–4
self-motivation 68
sensitivity, children's heightened 4
sensory avoidant behaviour 66
silence, periods of 58
social awareness 55
social balance 106–7
social comparison-making 41
social and emotional learning (SEL) 2
    benefits 9–10
    importance 4–15
    in the PYP classroom 8–9
social exclusion 40
social intelligence 51–5
social needs 32–6

social opportunities 32, 52
social skills 45–55
    and emotional intelligence 51–5
    modelling 45
    and social intelligence 51–5
    and wellbeing 40–2
social wellbeing 1–2, 6–9, 13, 106–8
society 34, 105
soundscapes, recording 62
speaking skills 56, 63–4, 96
stereotypes, gender 43
stress 75–84
    childhood 76–81
    signs of 77, 79
    work-related 5
stress management 78–81
    see also mindfulness
structure, provision 46, 60
student-led activities 86–7
student-teacher relationships 2, 13
surveys 99

T
TAILS see Teaching and Learning International Survey
Teacher Wellbeing Index 2019 5, 75
teachers
    and clothing 6
    and communication skills 43, 61
    and emails to parents 60, 66, 69, 73, 78–9
    and resilience 72
    and role-modelling 8–9, 19
    and self-criticism 87
    and stress 75–6
    and student-teacher relationships 2, 13
    and teamwork 7
    and wellbeing 2, 5, 6, 11–12
    and working hours 75–6
Teaching and Learning International Survey (TAILS) 76
teamwork 7
texture 37–8, 109–11
Thinkers 17, 22–3, 92–4

tongue-tied children 63
trains of thought 64
turn-taking 25, 96

U
uncertainty 30, 102

V
victimization, feelings of 41
viewpoints 26–8
visual information streams 61
visualization 80–1
volunteering 28

W
Walton, GM 40
Wechsler, David 20
wellbeing 1–2, 75, 85–6
    benefits of 9–10
    and classroom participation 12–13
    and communication skills 42–3
    definition 4–5
    and IB Leaner Profiles 16–39, 86
    importance 4–15
    physical 4–5, 6, 106–8
    practical strategies to foster 18–39
    in the PYP classroom 4–7
    and self-management skills 43–4
    social 1–2, 6–9, 13, 106–8
    and social skills 40–2
    strategies for implementing 10–14
    and student-teacher relationships 13
    teacher 5
wellbeing initiatives 85
    generating support for 7
    scheduling 13–14
    starting 11–12
work-related stress 5, 75–6
work/life balance 75–6
worksheets, IB Leaner Profile 88–111

Y
'yet', power of 30, 31
yoga 78, 81, 82, 83